EFFECTIVE
EDUCATION

Recent Titles in
Contributions to the Study of Education

EFFECTIVE EDUCATION

A Minority Policy Perspective

CHARLES VERT WILLIE

CONTRIBUTIONS TO THE STUDY OF EDUCATION, NUMBER 20

GREENWOOD PRESS

NEW YORK • WESTPORT, CONNECTICUT • LONDON

Library of Congress Cataloging-in-Publication Data

Willie, Charles Vert, 1927-
  Effective education.

  (Contributions to the study of education, ISSN
0196-707X ; no. 20)
  Bibliography: p.
  Includes index.
    1. Education—United States—Aims and objectives.
2. Education—United States—Evaluation. 3. Educational
planning—United States. 4. Afro-American universities
and colleges—Influence. I. Title. II. Series.
LA217.W55 1987   370'.973   86-14950
ISBN 0-313-25414-1 (lib. bdg. : alk. paper)

Library of Congress Catalog Card Number: 86-14950
ISBN: 0-313-25414-1
ISSN: 0196-707X

First published in 1987

Greenwood Press, Inc.
88 Post Road West, Westport, Connecticut 06881

Printed in the United States of America

∞™

The paper used in this book complies with the
Permanent Paper Standard issued by the National
Information Standards Organization (Z39.48-1984).

10 9 8 7 6 5 4 3 2 1

Copyright Acknowledgments

Grateful acknowledgment is given for permission to reprint the following:

Chapter 4, "Alternative Routes to Excellence," was published in *Centerboard* 2, no. 2 (Fall 1984): 19-23. Permission to reprint was granted by the Center for Human Relations Studies of the University of Oklahoma.

Chapter 7 was published as "Leadership Development Programs for Minorities: An Evaluation" in *Urban Review* 16, no. 4 (1984): 209-17. Permission to reprint was granted by Agathon Press, Inc.

Chapter 8 was published as "A Theory of Liberation Leadership" in *Journal of Negro History* 68, no. 1 (Winter 1983): 1-7. Permission to reprint was granted by the Association for the Study of Negro Life and History.

Chapter 11 was published as "The Education of Benjamin Elijah Mays: An Experience in Effective Teaching" in *Teachers College Record* 84, no. 4 (Summer 1983): 955-62. Permission to reprint was granted by Teachers College Press of Columbia University.

Chapter 12 was published as "Good and Bad Teaching That Adults Remember: An Essay on Effective Education" in *Equity and Choice* 1, no. 3 (Spring 1985): 19-24, 32. Permission to reprint was granted by the Institute for Responsive Education, Boston University.

Dedicated to my daughter and sons:
Sarah, Martin, and James

Contents

Part IV: TEACHING AND LEARNING STRATEGIES

Part V: FUTURE PROJECTIONS

Preface

In social organization, there are dominant and subdominant people of power. Dominants, with their large numbers or superior resources, can block and implement social action, but subdominants are limited to going alone or casting a veto. To implement, they must persuade a proportion of the dominants or a sufficiently large coalition of subdominants to cooperate with them. Otherwise they must wait upon the dominants.

The dominants are strong and have might on their side. But might is not always right. Subdominants are necessary and essential in social organization as a source of self-correction. This is one of their essential functions, for the welfare of subdominants is protected only if the total system functions effectively. A pathological social system may benefit dominants but not subdominants simultaneously; however, a social system that benefits subdominants usually benefits dominants too.

In education and in other institutional actions, the participation of subdominants is necessary and essential in the development of effective programs. Nevertheless, few racial and ethnic minorities or other subdominant populations have been represented among members of the committees, commissions, councils, and task forces that have examined the status of education in the United States. By and large, the membership of such groups has been predominantly middle class, middle aged, male, and white. With limited direct experience of what will and will not work for population groups that differ from their own, educational experts such as these must conjecture about the beneficial outcomes of alternative approaches to teaching and learning for a variety of population groups.

Conjecturing is a common source of error in public policy making. What works for dominants may not work for subdominants. But dominants may not know that this is so. Since they control the decision-making structures of society—including investigative committees, commissions, and councils—they may project their own way of life upon others and make recommendations unwittingly that fulfill their interests but violate the interests of others. Thus, the absence of subdominants in significant numbers on the various groups that have recently examined our system of education is one basis for calling into question the universal applicability of some of their recommendations.

The perspectives of dominants and of subdominants necessarily are different, for the two groups complement each other. Dominants therefore are at risk when they function without the advice and consent of subdominants. If, according to the adage, a page of experience is worth a volume of logic, then the participation and perspective of people of dissimilar experience are essential components in social planning.

This book introduces a minority perspective missing from the majority-dominated study groups that have expressed opinions about the system of education in the United States. Minorities have been described as mirrors of the majority, the conscience of the community, and the source of societal self-correction. These and other functions they perform. They fulfill these functions effectively when their difference from dominants is recognized and accepted as valid and valuable.

The book should be of interest to a variety of specialists in education, especially policy makers and planners, multicultural curriculum specialists, desegregation experts, and scholars in educational sociology, educational anthropology, and the foundations of education. It sets forth a point of view that has been informed by years of experience in desegregated education planning and higher education teaching and administration.

Here, then, is an alternative view of education, an optimistic orientation that marches to the beat of a different drummer. It emphasizes adequacy rather than excellence as an institutional requirement and stresses inclusiveness over exclusiveness. Individual enhancement and community advancement are identified as the dual goals of education. It is a point of view that links morality and ethics in education and that reminds all of the significance of suffering, sacrifice, and service—the real outcomes of a real education.

Acknowledged with appreciation is a grant from the Maurice Falk Medical Fund, which assisted in the preparation of the manuscript for publication. Also acknowledged are editorial consultation rendered by Katharine O. Parker and clerical assistance by Betty Blake.

EFFECTIVE EDUCATION

Part I

CONCEPTS, GOALS, AND POLICIES

1
Introduction:
Effective Education,
a Moral Enterprise

Langdon Gilkey, a U.S. citizen, spent two years in a civilian internment camp in Asia while the United States was at war with Japan. He went to Asia to teach English and kept during his period of internment a rather lengthy journal published under the title *Shantung Compound* (1966). He wrote down every fact and happening, every problem and its resolution that came to his attention.

In his internment camp were close to 2,000 people—Americans, British, Italians, Belgians, Dutch, Cubans, Russians, and a few others. They were of varying ages, sex categories, social status levels, occupations, and religions. Herded together in captivity in a small compound for the duration of the war, these disparate people had to work their way through their demographic barriers to reach their common humanity if they would survive.

In tension-filled and stress-producing situations, Gilkey learned something about education that he was never taught at Harvard, where he received an A.B. degree, or in elementary and secondary school. He learned that "when the . . . security of the self is threatened, the mind simply ceases to be [an] objective instrument. . . . It does not weigh the rational arguments on both sides of an issue and coolly direct a submissive ego to adopt the 'just and wise solution' " (Gilkey 1966:93). Such a picture of the mind as rational and objective, states Gilkey, "is a myth of the academics accustomed to dealing with theoretical problems in study or the laboratory rather than existential problems of life as it is lived" (Gilkey 1966:93).

Gilkey discovered that "technological advance spells progress only if people are in fact rational and good" and that people are rational and good only when they are able to sacrifice that which is precious and which they may need for their own existence. This means that to "be just or generous is by no means easy or natural." Because of the self-sacrifice that virtue requires, "it hurts rather than pays to be good" (Gilkey 1966:92).

This is an age in which technologies are exalted and admired. In this connection, I invite you to associate yourself with Gilkey's conclusion that "a [person] . . . subject to brutal or vicious prejudices, . . . [and who can harm others] with ease if one's security is threatened, is no technologist in whom to have confidence" (Gilkey 1966:95).

Based on understandings derived from Gilkey's prison camp experience, I assert that education is a moral enterprise and involves analysis and action—not one or the other but both. The world is full of people who know what is right but who do not have the courage to do what is right. Such people are not well educated, regardless of the grades they receive. It is immoral to know but not do what is right.

Several decades ago when Martin Luther King, Jr., was a freshman student at Morehouse College in Atlanta, Georgia, its president, Benjamin Mays, said: "It will not be sufficient for Morehouse College . . . to produce clever graduates, [people] fluent in speech and able to argue their way through; but rather honest [people], [people] who can be trusted in public and private—[people] who are sensitive to the wrongs, the sufferings, and the injustices of society and who are willing to accept responsibility for correcting [them]" (quoted in Willie and Edmonds 1978:13). In this passage, Mays established a set of priorities in which honesty, a cultivated characteristic, is more valued than verbal facility and in which doing what is right is as important as knowing what is right. Education ought to teach students to think and encourage students to act. People ought to know the truth and act accordingly. Later, during the Montgomery bus boycott, King acted on the words he had heard from this college president whom he called his spiritual mentor.

Learning how to serve, to suffer, and to sacrifice are the essence of an effective education. Philosopher John Rawls has stated the case for sacrifice well. He has written that none merits greater natural capacity or deserves a more favorable starting place. These are gifts of nature. "Those who have been favored by nature . . . may gain from their good fortune only on terms that improve the situation of those who have lost out" (Rawls 1971:101-4). In other words, an effective education is an education that teaches one how to serve, sacrifice, and suffer for others, to give them compensating advantages if necessary.

The success of any person is due in part to circumstances for which none can really claim full credit. Hard work, of course, is sometimes associated with success. People who work hard tend to attribute their success to this fact. But some people are successful who never had to work, and some who work have never been successful. "Success," said Nietzsche, "has always been a great liar" (quoted in Schlesinger 1972:62). Thus, to be well educated is to cultivate habits of service, to practice sacrifice, and to learn how to suffer. These are the outcomes of success that are mediated by an effective education. Success is not an end in itself—and neither is education. In summary, one who is well educated and successful is a "person for others" (Bosanquet 1968:271).

Being a person for others is better than being a master of others. Those who aspire to control others fully eventually are controlled by those over whom they would rule. It is a fundamental law of life that one cannot deny freedom to another without eventually enslaving oneself. A well-educated person has no wish to rule the lives of others.

This brings me to advice that seldom is given. Learn how to learn from your losses and from losers. To achieve success, one must risk failure. Most of us fail more often that we succeed. Life for all is filled with more opportunities missed than moments seized. And so it is fitting that our institutions of learning should teach us how to handle failure as well as success.

Theodore Isaac Rubin, a psychiatrist, said: "We must fight for the right to lose. If we don't accept the right to lose, then we so fear failure that we curtail realistic and attainable desires." Despite this obvious reality, said the psychiatrist, "our culture stands rigidly against failure and loss, looks upon loss . . . as an insult to the human condition" (Rubin 1975:206).

A psychologist studied two groups of male adolescents, a late-maturing group and an early-maturing group. The late-maturing young people were relatively small and slenderly built; they were relatively weak and below average in athletic ability; they were described as childish, relatively tense, and less "good looking." The early-maturing youngsters were markedly superior in strength and physical skill as well as physical attractiveness; they were well built, muscular, athletic, attractive, and more relaxed in social situations.

The people in both groups, when studied fifteen years later in their early thirties, had erased almost all their differences. Differences in gross size for the two groups had almost disappeared. There was no significant difference in average education received by the two groups and no difference in socioeconomic status attained. The same proportion in each group was married, and parents in each group had a similar number of children (Jones 1960:804-22). All this suggests that those who appear to be failures in one season may be successful in another and that the race of life does not belong to the swift but to those who endure.

In getting knowledge from computers and other forms of new technology, a well-educated person gains wisdom from the old traditions. The two go well together. Such a person remembers that "questions of good and evil, even if they lie outside the province of science cannot be considered to lie outside the province of the scientist." As stated by economist E. F. Schumacher, "There is no science without scientists" (Schumacher 1977:106). Early on in an educational career, one is encouraged to ask and answer the question about what one should do in life. As year succeeds to year, one should ask and begin to answer the question why one does what one should do. If education is a moral enterprise, questions of *what* and *how* should be linked with questions of *why*. An effective education enables one to relax, move ahead in one's own time, choose one's own drumbeat and if necessary ignore that of others, not to fear failure, and to be a person for others. Effectively educated people are wise but meek. The arrogant are consumed by their own conceit. Humility and wisdom go well together. The wise also are compassionate and caring.

REFERENCES

Bosanquet, Mary. 1968. *The Life and Death of Dietrich Bonhoeffer*. New York: Harper.

Gilkey, Langdon. 1966. *Shantung Compound*. New York: Harper.

Jones, Mary Cover. 1960. "The Late Careers of Boys Who Were Early or Late Maturing." In Jerome Seidman, ed., *The Adolescent*, pp. 804-22. New York: Holt, Rinehart, and Winston.

Rawls, John. 1971. *A Theory of Justice*. Cambridge, Mass.: Harvard University Press.

Rubin, Theodore Isaac. 1975. *Compassion and Self-Hate*. New York: Ballantine Books.

Schlesinger, Arthur, Jr. 1972. "The Power of Positive Losing." *New York Times Magazine* (June 22).

Schumacher, E. F. 1977. *A Guide for the Perplexed*. New York: Harper.

Willie, Charles Vert, and Ronald R. Edmonds, eds. 1978. *Black Colleges in America*. New York: Teachers College Press.

2

The Excellence Movement
and Lessons from History

The excellence movement in education in the United States is sanctioned by an authority as high as the federal government. In its report, *A Nation at Risk* (1983), the National Commission on Excellence in Education advocated raising college admissions requirements and the nationwide administration of standardized tests between high school and college and at other transitional points. The report considered these recommendations to be for the public welfare and identified the federal government as the most responsible agency to indicate the national interest in education (National Commission 1983: 27-28, 33). In addition to advocating standards, these recommendations encourage rejection of learners considered less worthy. I need not remind human development professionals of the impact that rejection has on the human personality.

In discussing the implications of the excellence movement, one must consider concepts of community psychology that have to do with freedom, equality, supremacy, preeminence, authority, responsibility, duty, obligation, acceptance, rejection, corruption, and violence. These concepts have to do with individuals interacting with others. These concepts involve persons as well as collectivities. They recognize that a proper understanding of individual behavior requires an understanding of the institutions and groups with which one is or is not affiliated.

Essentially excellence is a function of personal aspiration and accomplishment and therefore is a property of the individual. When excellence is conceived of as a property of the collectivity, an inappropriate transformation has occurred, and the possibility of abuse is present.

Collectivities may be held accountable as to whether they are performing in an appropriate way—that is, whether they encourage persons to serve others and whether they support individuals who serve, sacrifice, and suffer for the sake of others. Institutions, groups, and other collectivities are obligated to help individuals perform these functions adequately. Adequate individuals may aspire to excel. This aspiration is their privilege—a personal privilege and not a social obligation. Thus I conclude that the excellence movement that attempts to transform a personal privilege into a social obligation is inappropriate, misguided, and ultimately harmful. Such a movement is harmful because of the damaging social consequences that may result from it. To gain perspective on what happens when individuals begin to aspire for preeminence, which is synonymous with excellence, let us consult the record of ancient history. Book VI of the *Histories of Rome* written by Polybius, a Greek citizen who died in 118 B.C., is instructive (Polybius 200-118 B.C.).

Polybius, born around 200 B.C., had a wide experience of Roman political and military life. But as a Greek citizen, he was largely free from Roman national prejudice. Thus he was better able to search for truth, according to Betty Radice (Polybius 200-118 B.C. "Preface," 1). From 211 B.C. on, Rome was moving toward domination of the whole Hellenistic world (Polybius 200-118 B.C. "Introduction," 11). Polybius believed that if one wishes to pass judgment on the characters of good or evil people, "one should . . . examine their actions . . . at times of conspicuous success or failure" (Polybius 200-118 B.C. 9:302). We know that Rome as an empire not only succeeded but also failed. Polybius chronicled the happenings as Rome rose to world power. A review of this chronicle reveals events inherent in the success of Rome that also contributed to its failure. Such a review might help the United States, a world power, recognize events within its highly successful society that could lead eventually to its failure. In my judgment, the excellence movement is one such happening. It represents the striving for preeminence.

It is strange that the United States, which has achieved almost universal education at elementary and secondary levels, is so unhappy with this miraculous accomplishment as to pronounce it mediocre and to contend that because of this accomplishment the nation is gravely at risk. Such gross dissatisfaction with such a great accomplishment is a puzzlement. The National Commission on Excellence in Education appears to be critical of the educational system for becoming too inclusive and suggests in its recommendations that higher education should be saved from this fate by becoming more exclusive. Our institutions of higher education tend to gain prestige by boasting of the number of student applicants for admission who are rejected. My contention is that the inclusiveness of the educational system has been its greatest benefit. An informed and educated population is better capable of effective participation in the affairs of a democratic society. Not so, state the leaders of the educational establishment who served on the commission.

They view our past educational practices with alarm and warn that we must change our inclusive ways. In the United States, our leaders have not been able "to bear . . . with dignity the most complete transformation of [our educational] fortune" (Polybius 200-118 B.C. 302), from a closed and exclusive system to an open and inclusive system. The capacity to deal with this complete transformation of fortune is what Polybius called the "test of true virtue" (Polybius 200-118 B.C. 302). Our society seems to be failing this test in the doubt it has cast on the value of our transforming achievement of universal education by labeling it mediocre.

The call for excellence shifts the concern of formal education away from the twofold goal of individual enhancement and community advancement to that of personal development only. Such an emphasis fuels the flames of narcissism that threaten our society by eradicating a sense of community and mutuality. I trace the overemphasis on the individual and the underemphasis on the collectivity to the U.S. Supreme Court decisions in the mid-1950s that outlawed segregation in education. Obligated by law to provide equal educational access for all, establishment leaders began to discuss the entitlements of selected individuals. Daniel Bell, for example, said that postindustrial society is a meritocracy where high-scoring individuals on standardized tests should be brought to the top to make the best use of their talents (Bell 1973: 607-8). This is an elitist orientation that could have serious negative consequences. This attitude is contrary to that of Thomas Jefferson, who believed that education should equip all citizens with enough wisdom and virtue to manage common community concerns (Jefferson 1813: 114). Bell's statement carries a clear implication that high status and great responsibility in society should be reserved for those who have attained excellence.

Polybius, based on his observations of Rome, said that subsequent generations of authority holders reared in privilege will tend to "abandon their high responsibility . . . in favor of avarice . . . and excesses that go with it" (Polybius 200-118 B.C.: 308). It is highly probable that those reared in an atmosphere of privilege and entitlement will manifest high scores of excellence since achievement and privilege are correlated. Thus, the meritocratic formula for selecting leaders Bell advocated in subsequent years would perpetuate opportunities for some and exclude others from positions of high status and social responsibility in an arbitrary and capricious way. The experience of arbitrary inclusion or exclusion from public positions of authority because of a personal attribute of excellence is the matter at issue.

Polybius reminds us that "those who have gained access to leadership because of their personal attributes will cease to value equality and freedom and seek to raise themselves above their fellow citizens." Subsequent generations of such leaders, according to Polybius, will begin to "hanker after office . . . to seduce and corrupt the people in every possible way." Moreover, "through their senseless craving for prominence, they stimulate among the masses . . . an appetite for bribes and the habit of receiving them" (Polybius 200-118 B.C.: 309). Finally, Polybius reports that those who become accustomed to succeeding at the expense of others will eventually find a leader sufficiently ambitious to do their bidding. Such a leader tends to introduce a regime based on violence that banishes and despoils opponents. In turn, the state degenerates into bestiality (Polybius 200-118 B.C.: 309). This is what happened in the Roman state that "formed, grew . . . reached its zenith [and changed] for the worse" (Polybius 200-118 B.C.: 309).

At this time of conspicuous success in the education system of the United States, character in the people is found wanting. Instead of glorying in the nation's success of achieving universal education, we have begun to grumble about the education that each person receives, especially those who feel that theirs should be a preeminent education.

Movement from concern about community advancement to individual enhancement is in accord with the predictions of Polybius. The revolution for human dignity in the United States is marked by the end of the Civil War. Our national leaders of education and other institutions are the children and grandchildren of the founders of the revolution. Polybius discovered in ancient Rome that "as soon as a new generation has succeeded and the democracy falls into the hands of the grandchildren of its founders, they have become by this time so accustomed to equality and freedom . . . that they cease to value them" (Polybius 200-118 B.C.: 309).

Knowing what causes a nation to be at risk, we should be able to prevent the degeneration of our society in our times. The educational system will be strengthened by maintaining its twofold goal of community advancement and individual enhancement rather than focusing on only one or the other. This complex goal can be maintained by the practice of inclusiveness rather than exclusiveness in schools and other educational institutions. We know that a polymorphic population is better capable of surviving in a changing environment than is one that is homogeneous. Those who survive are by their experience quality members of the species. But high-quality individuals alone cannot save society. Thus high quality and diversity are linked and so are diversity and adequacy, circumstances the excellence movement does not comprehend.

REFERENCES

Bell, Daniel. 1973. "On Meritocracy and Equality." In Jerome Karabel and A. H. Halsey, eds., *Power and Ideology in Education*, pp. 607-35. New York: Oxford University Press.

Jefferson, Thomas. 1813. "Letters from Thomas Jefferson to John Adams on
    Natural Aristocracy." In Stuart Gerry Brown, ed., *We Hold These Truths*,
    pp. 114-18. New York: Harper, 1941.
National Commission on Excellence in Education. 1983. *A Nation at Risk*. Wash-
    ington, D.C.: U.S. Government Printing Office.
Polybius. 200-118 B.C. From Ian Scott-Kilvert, trans., *Polybius: The Rise of the
    Roman Empire*. New York: Penguin Books, 1980.

3
Education and
Public Policy

With the publication of *A Nation at Risk* (April 1983), members of the National Commission on Excellence in Education ushered in a season of reports that are for the purpose of helping to "define the problems afflicting American education" (National Commission 1983:vii). Despite the spate of reports that have followed *A Nation at Risk*, no national consensus has emerged regarding what ought to be done with respect to education. My guess is that consensus has not emerged because education has been defined as a problem rather than as an opportunity; and the reports are more concerned with excluding rather than including all sorts and conditions of people in all levels of the educational system.

The call for excellence in education is a code word for exclusiveness in education; make no mistake about this. These are examples of recommendations that ultimately could exclude. As mentioned in Chapter 2, the National Commission on Excellence in Education recommended that colleges and universities raise their admissions requirements, that standardized tests be administered regularly nationwide at transition points in an educational career such as from high school to college (National Commission 1983:27, 28, 33).

At a time when the proportion of college-enrolled blacks has increased from a recent low of 4.6 percent in 1965 to a 1982 high of 10 or 11 percent, why does the commission advocate higher admissions standards for institutions of higher education if it wishes to maintain this high level of matriculation for minorities? At a time when social scientists acknowledge that standardized tests may be less accurate predictors of the capacity of minorities to succeed in college and when they confess that measures of success in higher education are not necessarily measures of success in life (Schrader 1971:118), why does the commission recommend the regular administration of standardized achievement tests nationwide to certify all students if it wishes to be fair to minorities as well as the majority?

As a keystone to its recommendations for exclusiveness, the commission assigned the primary responsibility for identifying the national interest in education to the federal government. If the commission wishes to maintain an inclusive educational system, why assign the government the basic responsibility of defining the national interest in education when that government during the Reagan administration has refused to promote desegregated public schooling, has opposed affirmative action hiring, and is unsympathetic to bilingual education? Such a federal government cannot be trusted to identify the public interest in education for a nation that has a pluralistic population. I prefer to repose the ultimate authority for identifying the public interest in education in the people and not in the federal government.

Rather than viewing education with alarm, as do most of the contemporary reports, we should be celebrating the achievement of an inclusive and universal system of education in this nation where all sorts and conditions of people are served. Race, gender, and handicapped status continue as barriers to full participation in education, but they are less significant today as barriers than they have been in the past.

The universal education that this nation has attained at elementary and secondary levels is a remarkable achievement in history. The school enrollment rate for children five through seventeen years of age is nine out of every ten individuals; and the dropout rate for high school age youth in their junior and senior years is less than 8 percent (U.S. Bureau of the Census, 1984a:147, 160). There were 47 million people in elementary and secondary public and private schools in 1982, representing about one-fifth of the total population. That society was willing to spend $200.8 billion in 1982, a typical year, for education that directly benefited only one out of five of its members is an altruistic action (U.S. Bureau of the Census, 1984b:3). I hesitate to call it a generous act because the outlay for education in 1982 was only 6.5 percent of the gross national product (U.S. Bureau of the Census, 1984b:3, 5). The proportionate outlay for education should have been larger.

Despite recent gains in universal education at primary and secondary levels, the reports indicate that some leaders in education now doubt that all schools and all grade levels should be as inclusive as they have been. There are suggestions in *A Nation at Risk* and in other reports that schooling ought to be more exclusive, especially in higher grade levels. That this is the direction toward which we are tending is indicated by the language in commission's report, which describes the contemporary educational system as a "rising tide of mediocrity" (National Commission 1983:5).

It is strange that the system of education in the United States that sent one-third of its high school graduates to college in 1982, compared with slightly less than one-fourth approximately two decades earlier, is classified as in a "current declining trend" (National Commission 1983:15). Certainly the trend has not declined for women, who nearly doubled their proportions in college between 1960 and 1982. Women going to college increased from 17.9 percent to 31.8 percent of all female high school graduates during this twenty-two-year period. College-going blacks also increased substantially from 18.4 percent in 1960 to 28 percent in 1982 of all black high school graduates (U.S. Bureau of the Census 1984a:160). Today there are more than 105 women to every 100 men enrolled in college; in 1970 there were only 70 women to every 100 men in college (U.S. Bureau of the Census, 1984a:162). Today black students enrolled in college are 10 or 11 percent, a proportion similar to that for blacks in the total population, which is 11 or 12 percent; in 1970 the proportion of blacks in college was only 5 percent. This proportion was only half that for blacks in the nation, which was 10 or 11 percent at that time (U.S. Bureau of the Census 1984a:162, 1984b:1).

If there has been a decline in the higher education system in recent years, it has been in the proportion of white males among college students. In 1960 a majority of all students in college were white males; today they are a minority (U.S. Bureau of the Census 1984a:160). Could it be that the National Commission, overwhelmingly white and male, classified the current educational system as mediocre and in a declining state because it no longer caters exclusively or in a disproportionate way to the interests and concerns of white males? This is an interesting question to ponder in the light of the evidence that the higher education sector of the system today includes a higher proportion of women and a higher proportion of racial minorities than it did in the past.

The United States has achieved a democratic educational system more open and more equal than ever that is condemned as mediocre by those who no longer exclusively control it. Those who condemn the system see that this system does not serve their interests now as a priority concern but serves the interests of others of lesser status too.

The current critics of education are playing a trick on women and all minorities, not unlike the trick played on blacks years ago. When they were down on the farm, blacks were told that to get ahead, they had to quit their countrified ways, go the city, and become urbane. As blacks began to pour into urban areas to seek their fortunes, whites changed the name of the get-ahead game and declared that cities had disintegrated, that cities were dead, and that only the suburbs provided livable environments. This, of course, was a premature and false obituary for cities. Without a vital central city, suburban communities cannot survive. But no one told blacks that this was so. Blacks were led to believe that they had inhabited irrelevant urban relics of the past, especially when they began to be elected as mayors.

A democratic freedom-loving nation that has established a constitutional democracy, which requires equity in the distribution of educational resources and equality of access to these resources, should be pleased with this accomplishment. Instead it is described by eighteen learned leaders (members of the National Commission) as being an educational system that "threatens our very future as a Nation and as a people" (National Commission 1983:5).

I declare that the commission's assessment is wrong because it did not understand the goals of good education. A primary characteristic of good education is diversity in the learning environment. Diversified human resources in a truth-seeking institution help that institution to become self-correcting. Where there is diversity, there are dominant and subdominant people of power, sometimes called majority and minority populations, who embrace each other in a complementary way. When schools, colleges, and universities are appropriately diversified—that is, when ideally the majority is not greater than two-thirds and the minority is one-third or never less than the minimum effective critical mass of one-fifth—the participants in such a system are obligated to seek a double victory that mutually benefits minorities as well as the majority. A double victory is consistent with the concept of community that seeks to transform the enemy into a friend. Where there is a double victory, all win and none loses. The adversary is not victimized, humiliated, and vanquished because subdominants as well as dominants recognize that persons in each group are necessary and essential.

Many reports describe education and its outcomes in personalistic terms only, such as years in school completed, grade point average, rank in class, standardized test score percentile, skills developed, jobs obtained. These outcomes of education for individuals are important. But education, as defined by Benjamin Mays, ought to do more than develop individuals fluent in speech. It ought to do more than cultivate mental agility in the manipulation of mathematical symbols. According to Mays, education ought to teach a society how to eliminate poverty, overcome oppression, and achieve justice (cited in Willie 1978:13). These functions of education complement those of individual development. These are functions of group and community betterment. Thus education has this twofold goal in society: personal enhancement and community advancement. One dimension without the other is incomplete; the two ought always to be kept together in a complementary way.

The principle of complementarity alerts us to the presence always of two norms: the norm of dominant and the norm of subdominant people.

In complementary relationships, there is no intrinsic value in being either dominant or subdominant. Each is mutually dependent on the other for mutual survival. None, however, ought always to be dominant or subdominant in all situations. There is evidence of an emerging perception of the principle of complementarity in our contemporary educational system. But we see this principle through a glass darkly; our understanding of it is partial.

The National Commission said that "public commitment to excellence . . . must [not] be made at the expense of . . . public commitment to the equitable treatment of our diverse population" (National Commission 1983:13). But the report did not tell how to achieve equity while striving for excellence.

My judgment is that excellence and equity are improperly linked. Excellence has to do with individual aspiration. Equity is a property of community organization. Excellence and equity have to do with different dimensions of society—its individual and group dimensions—and should not be linked as the commission attempted to do. To treat excellence and equity as variables of a similar order is to embrace confusion.

I do not oppose excellence in education. Any individual who identifies excellence as a personal goal and who works diligently to achieve it does a commendable thing. Those who achieve excellence in any life experience often sacrifice personal privileges and pleasures for its attainment. Let us clearly recognize, however, that excellence is an individual and not an institutional goal.

An institution cannot require any individual affiliated with it to be excellent. An institution has not the right to require sacrifice of personal pleasures by individuals for the attainment of excellence. Self-sacrifice is a property of the individual; it is a moral decision and should never be surrendered to collective control. Institutions are concerned with what is ethical and fair for the collectivity. Institutions of education may require that all affiliated with them be adequate or competent, that those whom they certify are good enough to help and not harm others. This is their ethical obligation to society, a responsibility that legitimately belongs to the collectivity.

Individual rights and group requirements are not the same. Because of this I assert that excellence, a moral aspiration of the individual, and equity, an ethical requirement of the group, are improperly linked in the report of the commission.

It is appropriate to classify the diminishing discrimination in educational opportunities by race and gender as a significant trend in educational equity of the second half of the twentieth century. Legal sanction for sexist and racist practices in education has eroded but not disappeared in recent years. Despite these gains against discrimination, schools and other learning environments have not attained the full status of just institutions.

We have not achieved a just system of schooling because elitism has taken over where racism and sexism left off and is performing some of the racist and sexist "dirty work" under the banner of maintaining high standards. If racism and sexism are diminishing trends in elementary and secondary education, elitism is a trend that is increasing in higher education.

Consider this fact: As one ascends the ladder of higher education, the proportions of racial minorities and women tend to decrease. Education, of course, is the fastest elevator to upward mobility in the United States. Education probably makes a greater contribution to opportunities for individuals than do family background and other attributes of social origin of subdominant people in the United States. A majority of parents in all racial populations now wish for a college education for their children. And the aspiration level for such an education is even higher among blacks than among whites. Why, then, is the black proportion of all students in graduate school lower than the black proportion of all students in junior colleges?

This is where elitism comes in. In the name of high standards, the elitist attempts to exclude subdominants and reserves the higher levels of education and its benefits for the dominant people of power. Elitism is the artificial reservation of opportunities and benefits for some people who may be less effective than others who have been excluded in an arbitrary way. We know, for example, that 87 percent of all blacks admitted to medical schools graduate and become competent physicians although their standardized test scores average 100 points less than the average for whites (Willie 1982:305). Such scores obviously are not a good prediction of who among different racial groups is capable of being a good physician.

We persist in trying to find the brightest and the best. E. F. Schumacher said, "The idea of competition, natural selection, and the survival of the fittest" is one of six leading ideas from the nineteenth century that continues to dominate the minds of educated people today (Schumacher 1973:88).

By assuming that some people are more fit than all others for all occasions, the elitists act toward women and minorities in ways that sexists and racists would not be permitted to act today. They exclude women and minorities ceremonially, using arbitrary means such as standardized test scores that appear to be just but in essence are unfair—first because the tests are made by and standardized on a dominant population and second because blacks in the United States, particularly in integrated situations, seem to have a different temporal pattern of learning and development. Blacks begin slowly but may end victoriously. In the Scriptures, it is written: "Better is the end of a thing, than the beginning thereof" (Ecclesiastes 7:8). The standardized aptitude test scores predict only the first-year performance in college, graduate, or professional school. But first-year performance is not a good indication of the capacity of blacks and other subdominant populations to do demanding educational work. The fourth-year performance of blacks is sometimes better than is that of whites (Willie and McCord 1972:86-87).

If, according to the principle of complementarity, there is not one norm but always two norms in society that are valid, then an aptitude test standardized on a majority population is an inappropriate tool of assessment for a minority population whose norms and goals necessarily are different but complementary. The increased significance such tests have attained in the admissions decisions of schools of good learning is a deliberate elitist attempt by dominants to exclude subdominants from the privileges and benefits of college and graduate school.

As we move through the second half of the twentieth century, two trends in education are manifested: a trend toward inclusiveness that emphasizes justice and a trend toward exclusiveness that emphasizes excellence.

Subdominants fought against discrimination and for justice in our educational system, and dominants fought against mediocrity and for excellence in the system. Excellence that promotes injustice is unworthy, and so is justice that tolerates and encourages mediocrity. Mediocrity and injustice harm and do not help people. To protect against injustice and mediocrity in education, the participation of both dominants and subdominants is needed.

If we accept the fact that both dominants and subdominants are essential in social organizations, including educational institutions, then I predict that a new trend will emerge in education. Neither dominants who promote exclusiveness nor subdominants who promote inclusiveness will have their way.

With a genuine desire to achieve excellence as the thesis and a genuine belief in inclusiveness as the antithesis, schools of the future probably will be neither places of excellence nor settings of mediocrity, especially those with dominant and subdominant populations that complement each other. Such schools of the future are likely to be learning environments that are adequate, with competent and sufficient people. Educated people who are adequate may be neither the brightest and the best nor the dullest and the worst. They are sufficient to the requirements of situations in which they find themselves. Who could ask that any person be more than sufficient? Adequate individuals are sufficiently equipped to help and not harm those whom they serve. Adequacy will emerge as a synthesis goal of education in a pluralistic society. Such a compromise is inevitable in schools of a pluralistic democratic society.

Adequacy among scholars is one consequence of democracy. Ultimately this may be better than the excellence that a despot may attempt to decree or the mediocrity tolerated by the anarchist.

In the family, many are called to be parents and children. None is perfect; few are excellent; most are merely adequate or good enough. Why should teachers and students in schools be different? It was Daniel Levinson who said that when one no longer feels that one must be remarkable, one is free to be oneself (Levinson et al. 1978:251)—which is to say, one is contented with being adequate—good enough to help and not harm others. Excellence is fine and beautiful. But adequacy is good enough.

REFERENCES

Fletcher, Joseph. 1960. *Situation Ethics*. Philadelphia: Westminster Press.

Levinson, Daniel J., et al. 1978. *The Seasons of a Man's Life*. New York: Ballantine Books.

National Commission on Excellence in Education. 1983. *A Nation at Risk*. Washington, D.C.: U.S. Government Printing Office.

Polybius. 200-118 B.C. From Ian Scott-Kilvert, trans., *Polybius: The Rise of the Roman Empire*. New York: Penguin Books, 1980.

Schrader, W. B. 1971. "The Predictive Validity of College Board Admissions Tests." In William H. Angoff, ed., *The College Board Admissions Testing Program*, pp. 117-45. New York: College Entrance Examination Board.

Schumacher, E. F. 1973. *Small Is Beautiful*. New York: Harper.

U.S. Bureau of the Census. 1984a. *Statistical Abstract of the United States, 1984*. Washington, D.C.: U.S. Government Printing Office.

_____. 1984b. *USA Statistics in Brief*. Washington, D.C.: Department of Commerce, Bureau of the Census.

U. S. Bureau of Labor Statistics. 1980. *Handbook of Labor Statistics*. Washington, D.C.: U.S. Government Printing Office.

Willie, Charles Vert. 1978. "Racism, Black Education, and the Sociology of Knowledge." In C. V. Willie and Ronald R. Edmonds, eds., *Black Colleges in America*, pp. 3-13. New York: Teachers College Press.

_____. 1982. "The Recruitment and Retention of Minority Health Professionals." *Alabama Journal of Medical Sciences* 19 (July): 303-8.

Willie, Charles Vert, and Arlene Sakuma McCord. 1972. *Black Students at White Colleges*. New York: Praeger.

Part II
ALTERNATIVE REALITIES

4
Alternative Routes
to Excellence

Humanity is a system of complementary actions. This is the source of its self-renewal, the basis of its transcendent possibility. Transcendency is our fuller reality. Yet we persist in our efforts at reductionism. In language, we often omit the feminine pronoun *she*, stating that it is included in the masculine pronoun *he*. Sociologist Joan Huber has appropriately observed that "to use 'men' to mean both 'men' and 'women and men' is an exercise in double-think" (Huber 1976:89). In our thinking, we try to reduce that which is abstract to that which is concrete. In our doing, we try to reduce possibilities to practicalities. We are most interested in developing unitary and efficient social systems.

According to the wisdom of Solomon, there is not one but two principal senses of inquiry—the eye and the ear. The eye is never satisfied with seeing nor the ear with hearing (quoted in Bacon 1624-1626:5). Both are important in the fullness of apprehension. Maybe our goal should be the development not of unitary social systems but of those with components that are complementary. Such are more likely to be effective, even if they are less likely to be efficient.

An ultimate form of reductionism is the subjugation of the wish and will of the subdominant or minority to the preeminent authority of the dominant or majority. There is no health in this kind of situation. The possibility of self-renewal in society is absence when disobedience to authority is not tolerated. Stanley Milgram, who conducted an experimental study on obedience and authority, reminds us that "the problem of obedience . . . is not wholly psychological. The form and shape of society . . . have much to do with it" (Milgram 1974:11).

If we wish to have an open society, a healthy society, and even a happy society, we must deliberately delimit the authority and power of individuals and institutions so that none can coerce others into conformity. Freedom also must have its way.

I am persuaded by the argument of Harvey Cox that "innovation . . . requires a *variety* of experiments going on, 'a hundred flowers blooming' " (Cox 1969:57). Let the leaders of education see and hear this fact and believe in it. Let the leaders of education beware: Their current concern about standards and their contemporary emphasis on excellence could reduce the number of flowers that bloom, thus damaging the knowledge base we passionately seek.

Knowledge both reveals and conceals; none has perfect knowledge; all knowledge is partial; the capacity for wonder is still a necessity, even among those who aspire to be excellent (Bacon 1624-1626:7). Therefore we should be slow to limit access to knowledge; we should not limit the paths to excellence. I say, let a hundred flowers bloom. Let a thousand flowers bloom. Let millions of flowers bloom.

In the book of our traditional wisdom, it is written that no one should put a stumbling block in another's way (Romans 14:13). Could it be that our standardized testing that favors some population groups over others is a stumbling block? Could it be that our admissions procedures that emphasize some mental abilities over others is a stumbling block? Regretfully a society with exclusive and elitist orientations does not ask or answer these questions so far as education is concerned.

Let me give a few examples of what happens when several different flowers are permitted to bloom. The results of my recent study, *Five Black Scholars*, are instructive (Willie 1986). John Hope Franklin is a specialist in history, an emeritus professor of the Department of History at the University of Chicago, where he occupied an endowed chair. He was born in Oklahoma, attended Fisk University, graduating magna cum laude, and enrolled in Harvard, where he earned a Ph.D. degree and forty years later was awarded an honorary doctoral degree. A founding member of the Phi Beta Kappa chapter at Fisk, Franklin eventually served as president of the Southern Historical Association, the American Historical Association, and the United Chapters of Phi Beta Kappa.

Franklin had a head start. His mother had a college education and was a teacher. He played on the back bench of her classroom when he was of preschool age and learned to read early by listening to the lessons his mother provided for others. His father also was college educated; he studied and practiced law. Franklin grew up in a family of professionals who urged him and his siblings to get an education. All finished college, following in the footsteps of their parents. John Hope Franklin was named in honor of the first black president of Morehouse College, a school his father attended. Surrounded by learned parents who provided a strong support system, Franklin's achievements were predictable outcomes of such an intellectually stimulating household. In my study, John Hope Franklin was identified as the preeminent black historian in the United States.

In that same study, Kenneth B. Clark was voted by a national sample of psychologists the most renowned black psychologist in the nation. But his path to excellence was quite different from that of Franklin. Clark was born in the Panama Canal Zone of parents who had migrated from Jamaica. When the marriage of his parents dissolved, he moved with his mother and his younger sister to New York City when he was four years old. His mother worked in the garment industry by day, attended night school, and eventually received a diploma. She gave full support to Clark and urged him and his sister to go to college. She cared for the family as well as she could, imprisoned in a big city ghetto where material rewards were hard to come by.

Clark graduated from Howard University and received a Ph.D. degree in psychology from Columbia University. For a third of a century, Clark taught at City College of New York. He retired as a Distinguished University Professor Emeritus. A member of Phi Beta Kappa and Sigma Xi, Clark also headed national professional associations in his discipline, including the American Psychological Association and the Society for the Psychological Study of Social Issues. In addition, Clark served for several years as an elected member of the powerful New York State Board of Regents.

There are similarities in the achievements of Franklin and Clark but gross differences in their backgrounds and pathways to excellence. Franklin came from a two-parent, middle-class family in which both parents were professionals. Clark grew up in a single-parent, working-class household in which his mother was the sole source of support. Working by day and going to school by night, Clark's mother could not provide constant supervision over a family whose children were coming of age in a big city ghetto.

Other differences have to do with their geographic origins and social experiences. Franklin was southern born and southern reared, and Clark was foreign born and northern reared. The risks, opportunities, dangers, and difficulties to which both scholars were exposed in Oklahoma and New York when they were growing up were quite different, as were their socioeconomic status. But these different circumstances and conditions seemed to have made no difference in their reputations; they followed different paths to honor and glory. Yet each man is an accomplished scholar. Franklin's and Clark's stories indicate that place of birth, family composition, socioeconomic status, education and occupation of parents, and region of residence may facilitate the achievement of excellence or serve as an impediment. Even when an impediment, they can be transcended. There are different paths to honor and glory as revealed in the lives of these great men.

Even more disparate than the life-styles of Franklin and Clark were the experiences of Matthew Holden, Jr., and Darwin T. Turner. Holden is a political scientist who occupies an endowed professorship at the University of Virginia in Charlottesville. Turner is a specialist in literature and a Distinguished Professor at the University of Iowa. Both scholars are in their fifties and have made significant contributions to the literature in their fields and to the professional associations of their disciplines.

Holden has been an elected member of the governing council of the American Political Science Association and has also served as its vice-president. In addition, he has served the Social Science Research Council as a board member and was appointed to the Assembly of Behavioral and Social Sciences of the National Academy of Science. Holden is also a public administrator and was commissioner of the Wisconsin Public Service Commission. He served in a similar capacity with the Federal Energy Regulatory Commission in Washington, D.C. He has been a faculty member at approximately five different schools.

Turner has been a member of the board of directors of the Modern Language Association and the National Council of Teachers of English. In addition, he is a trustee of the National Humanities Center. Turner also is an educational administrator and has served not only as department chair several times but also as an academic dean. He has been a professor or administrator at approximately six different schools.

Matthew Holden, Jr., was voted by a national sample of political scientists the most outstanding black scholar in that field in the nation; and Darwin Turner was voted by a national sample of literature scholars the most outstanding black specializing in literature. Beyond these striking similarities in career accomplishments at the mid-century mark in their lives, Holden's and Turner's pathways to honor and glory are radically different. The members of Holden's family of orientation were Mississippi farmers before joining the World War II migration of blacks to the city in search of jobs in industry. Turner came from a family of gifted intellectuals and professionals. His paternal grandfather was a college teacher; he also was a public school principal, as was his maternal grandmother. His parents were college graduates, as were some of his grandparents. His mother received a master's degree in education, and his father studied pharmacy. Both pursued professions connected with the training they received.

Turner's family earned bachelor's and master's degrees, and his paternal grandfather, whom Turner described as a great inspiration, was a Ph.D. graduate in biology from the University of Chicago, the school from which Turner also received his terminal academic degree. His maternal great-grandfather was one of the first black teachers in Cincinnati. Thus, education as a course of study and as a profession was part of the socialization experience of Turner. In this respect, his life was very much unlike that of Holden, whose parents were blue-collar workers on the farm and in the city.

Turner had a large extended family in the city, and so did Holden on the farm. There the similarity of their family experiences ended. Following crop failures, Holden's parents moved to Chicago to labor as unskilled workers. After finishing his studies in pharmacy, Turner's father moved to Chicago to establish three drugstores. His father commuted back to Cincinnati periodically, and his mother visited Chicago often. The burden of city life was too much for Holden's parents, both of whom had less than a high school education. Eventually they went separate ways. Holden remained in his mother's household, where, he said, there was bread enough but not much to spare.

Turner whizzed through school, completing college summa cum laude in three years and a master's degree at the University of Cincinnati two years later and earning a Phi Beta Kappa key. He had accomplished all of this by the age of eighteen years. Holden's baccalaureate degree was earned in a stop-and-go fashion—four years at the University of Chicago that he described as a great experience and also one that overwhelmed him. He failed to complete his B.A. degree there and finished two years later at Roosevelt University, also in Chicago. He earned a master's degree by the age of twenty-three. A stint in the armed forces and jobs with county and metropolitan planning or charter commissions delayed his study for the Ph.D. degree at Northwestern University, which Holden did not receive until he was twenty-nine. During this time, Holden was single and on his own. Turner interrupted his studies for the Ph.D. degree to teach in two colleges. The degree was awarded when he was twenty-five. Although he had a wife and child, Turner lived and studied in Chicago, where his father owned a business and could be turned to for assistance. Turner too was on his own, but he knew there was help available in time of trouble.

Despite differences in region of birth, childhood socialization experiences, education and occupation of parents, family composition, and personal educational progress, both Holden and Turner came out on top with professional reputations. Both have divided their careers between scholarship and administration. Both are high achievers in their respective disciplines. Both are living examples of the multiple routes to success.

In summary, the most outstanding black scholars in four fields grew up in a variety of family forms, including nuclear families and extended families, two-parent and single-parent households. The occupations of parents ranged from unskilled and semiskilled workers to professionals and self-employed business operators. Some parents failed to finish high school; others finished college and had graduate degrees too. Farm folk and cosmopolitan city dwellers these families were. They had northern and southern roots.'

These outstanding scholars had other varied experiences. One completed college in three years, two in four years, and one in six years. Two graduated from predominantly black colleges; two graduated from predominantly white colleges. One married before he was twenty; one married after he was thirty; two married at ages between these extremes. Two have taught in black and in white schools; two have taught extensively in predominantly white schools only. There are different roads to excellence, as the lives of these scholars reveal. One should be slow to emphasize conformity as standardized testing does, be slow to exclude the deviant, as the raising of admissions standards suggests.

In letting a hundred, a thousand, or a million flowers bloom, one acknowledges that in the human social system it is quantity that gives rise to quality, not the other way around. For this reason, the excluding prescriptions of the National Commission on Excellence in Education are wrong.

Sociologist Ezra Vogel reported that the "Japanese do not hesitate to overlap and duplicate their effort to gather relevant information. . . . The scope of government information-gathering is breath-taking." When an issue becomes salient, Japan assigns competing research projects to several institutes. In Japan, the quantity of information is the means by which that society reaches its quality decisions. The Japanese believe "this increases the chance of reaching a wise decision" (Vogel 1979:52).

In human animal society, a quality physical experience such as health, for example, is jeopardized in the presence of a quantity of unhealthy individuals. But in human transcendent society, excellent or quality solutions derive from a quantity of people thinking about them. Let us therefore adopt a transcendent educational philosophy of inclusiveness that encourages millions of flowers to bloom. Their petals shall mark the many different routes that lead to excellence and high quality.

REFERENCES

Bacon, Francis. 1624-1626. From *The Advancement of Learning*. London: J. M. Dent and Sons, 1973.

Cox, Harvey. 1969. "Feasibility and Fantasy: Sources of Social Transcendence." In Herbert Richardson and Donald L. Cutler, eds., *Transcendence*, pp. 53-63. Boston: Beacon Press.

Huber, Joan. 1976. "And Some Are More Equal Than Others." *American Sociologist* 2 (May): 85-95.

Mays, Benjamin E. 1983. *Quotable Quotes of Benjamin E. Mays*. New York: Vantage Press.

Milgram, Stanley. 1974. *Obedience to Authority*. New York: Harper.

Murphy, Michael. 1969. "Education for Transcendence." In Herbert W. Richardson and Donald L. Cutler, eds., *Transcendence*, pp. 18-30. Boston: Beacon Press.

National Commission on Excellence in Education. 1933. *A Nation at Risk*. Washington, D.C.: U.S. Government Printing Office.

Romans 14:13.

Smith, Houston. 1969. "The Reach and the Grasp: Transcendence Today." In Herbert W. Richardson and Donald L. Cutler, eds., *Transcendence*, pp. 1-17. Boston: Beacon Press.

U.S. Bureau of the Census. 1984. *Statistical Abstract of the United States, 1984*. Washington, D.C.: U.S. Government Printing Office.

Vogel, Ezra F. 1979. *Japan as Number One*. New York: Harper.

Willie, Charles Vert. 1986. *Five Black Scholars*. Cambridge, Mass.: Abt Books.

5
Relative Effects of Race, Gender, and Socioeconomic Status

During the closing years of the 1970s decade, I was a participant in the debate about the relative effects of race and social class on the life chances of various population groups. Another participant in that debate was William Wilson, who claimed that "the black middle class is enjoying unprecedented success in finding white collar jobs"; that "access to the means of production [various occupations] is increasingly based on education"; that the low-wage sector occupied by some blacks is not because of racial discrimination but due to their inferior education; and, finally, that "class has become more important than race in determining black life chances" (Wilson 1978:99, 151). Wilson's claims were contrary to those of Robert Hauser and David Featherman, who discovered that "racial discrimination in the process of stratification is primarily socioeconomic" (Hauser and Featherman 1977:xxv), and also the conclusion of Herman Miller that "race discrimination is a key cause" of blacks' perpetual low estate" (Miller 1965:21) and that "education does not do as much for [blacks and Hispanics] financially as it does for others" (Miller 1971:167).

During the course of the debate, I introduced a counterhypothesis that the "significance of race is increasing especially for middle-class blacks who, because of school desegregation and affirmative action and other integration programs, are coming into direct contact with whites for the first time for extended interaction" (Willis 1979:157). Also I pointed out that "education alone cannot explain the disproportionate number of blacks in low-paying jobs" since only half of the white population with an education limited to elementary school is employed in jobs of lowest prestige such as service workers and laborers, but four-fifths of blacks of similarly limited education work in these occupations (Willie 1979:154).

This chapter is a further contribution to the analysis of the relative effects of race and socioeconomic status on life chances; however, it deals with whites as well as blacks, assuming that a symbiotic relationship exists between dominant and subdominant populations. The effect of sex or gender is considered too.

DATA AND METHODS

Data for the analysis are the total employed population sixteen years of age and over in the United States. These data were obtained from several series produced by the U.S. Bureau of Labor Statistics and published in the 1980 *Handbook of Labor Statistics* (Bulletin 2070) (U.S. Labor Department 1980).

The analysis compares males and females, blacks and whites, and white males, white females, black males, and black females. The distribution of these race, sex, and race-sex categories in higher-prestige and lower-prestige occupational categories is compared along with the education that people in these categories have achieved. The higher-prestige category is of professionals, technical workers, managers, and administrators. The lower-prestige category includes skilled and semiskilled workers, service workers, and laborers (collectively called blue-collar workers). The higher-prestige category includes some but not all white-collar workers; however, the blue-collar category includes all lower-prestige occupations. In this study the socioeconomic indicator that differentiates these occupational categories is median year of education attained.

The measures used to describe the relative effects of race and gender on life chances are simple percentages, ratios, and averages. The ratios of observed to expected percentages are derived from a comparison of the percentage distribution of the total population in the labor force or of schooling to the percentage distribution of the population in selected occupational and educational categories. Ratios of the "ideal type" and deviations from it are constructed by assigning or designating the activity of white males as the expected experience and then relating it to the observed educational or occupational experiences of white females, black males, and black females. The proportion of the expected or ideal-type experience is the denominator, and the proportion of the observed or actual experience is the numerator in the calculation of ratios.

The decade from 1970 to 1979 is the study period; 1975 is designated as the middle year of the decade for determining the occupational distribution for various population groups.

Table 5.1
Distribution of Professional and Managerial Occupations
Within Race-Sex Groups, United States, 1975

	Percent		
	Professionals and	All Other	
Race-Sex Category	Managers	Occupations	Total
White male	29.9	70.1	100.0
White female	21.5	78.5	100.0
Black male	15.8	84.2	100.0
Black female	15.9	84.1	100.0

	Percent		
	Blue-collar	All Other	
Race-Sex Category	Workers	Occupations	Total
White male	46.9	53.1	100.0
White female	34.3	65.7	100.0
Black male	72.8	27.2	100.0
Black female	56.6	43.4	100.0

Source: U.S. Labor Department, Handbook of Labor Statistics,
  Washington, D.C.: U.S. Government Printing Office, 1980,
  p. 47.

FINDINGS

Table 5.1 reveals that 30 out of every 100 employed white males
(sixteen years of age and over) were high-status white-collar workers in
1975. They were employed as professionals, technical workers, managers, and administrators. This proportion is the highest of any of the
other race-sex categories. White males were followed immediately by
white females, of whom one-fifth worked in these high-status occupations. One-sixth of black males and a similar proportion of black females
were employed as professionals, technical workers, managers, and
administrators. Almost twice that proportion of white males, compared

with blacks, was employed in occupations of highest prestige in the United States.

Table 5.1 also reveals the employment experience of whites and of blacks in the lower-status, blue-collar occupations. A majority of blacks (57 percent of females and 73 percent of males sixteen years of age and over) in 1975 worked in the blue-collar sector of the labor force. This experience contrasts with that of whites, of whom a minority (both males and females) were blue-collar workers. The lowest proportion of blue-collar workers is found among white females (only one-third), and the highest proportion (nearly three-fourths) is among black males. The proportion of black males in the lower-prestige sector of occupations is almost twice as great as the proportion of whites in this sector.

The employment experience of black males in low-prestige, blue-collar occupations, compared to white females in these jobs, is similar to the employment experience of white males in high-prestige white-collar occupations, compared to black females in these jobs. Both male populations groups exceed by nearly twofold the proportion of females of the opposite race employed in these occupations. The only difference in these distribution patterns is that black males are joined by black females with a similarly low proportion of employment in high-status occupations, but white males are not joined by females with a similarly high proportion of employment in high-status occupations. In summary, white males stand alone at the top of the occupational hierarchy, having the largest proportion of employees in high-status occupations, and black males stand alone at the bottom of the occupational hierarchy, having the largest proportion of employees in low-status occupations.

These findings indicate that whatever successes blacks were having in 1975 in finding white-collar jobs was still less than expected, whether or not it was "unprecedented," as Wilson claimed. The observed proportions of black males and black females in occupations of highest status are 38 to 39 percent less than expected, if distributions were similar to their proportions of employed in the total labor force (Table 5.2). The black experience of underrepresentation in high-status occupations is a contrast to that of white males, who are overrepresented in such occupations; however, black women and black men are proportionately greater than expected in blue-collar occupations.

Table 5.3 indicates that differences in occupational experience by race between 1970 and 1979 hardly could be attributed to differences in education. The average median grade completed by blacks and by whites in blue-collar jobs during the 1970s differs by less than one school year. The same is true of blacks and whites in white-collar jobs. High school graduation is the prevailing experience for adults in racial majority and minority populations and for males and females. Certainly this was their experience toward the close of the 1970s.

Table 5.2
Total Population, White-Collar and Blue-Collar Occupations,
By Race-Sex Categories, United States, 1975

Race-Sex Category	Total Population Employed 16 Years and Over (in thousands)	Percent			Ratio	
		Total Population Employed	Total Professionals and Managers[a]	Total Blue-Collar Workers[b]	% Observed to Expected for Professional Manager	% Observed to Expected for Blue-Collar
White male	46,284	54.6	64.1	57.6	1.17	1.05
White female	29,429	34.7	29.3	26.7	.84	.77
Black male	4,947	5.8	3.6	9.5	.62	1.64
Black female	4,124	4.9	3.0	6.2	.61	1.27
Total	84,784	100.0	100.0	100.0	1.00	1.00

[a] N = 21,621

[b] N = 37,736

Source: U.S. Labor Department, Handbook of Labor Statistics, Washington, D.C.: U.S. Government Printing Office, 1980, pp. 141-146.

Table 5.3
Median School Year Completed for People Employed as Professionals and Managers and as Blue-Collar Workers By Race and Sex Categories, United States, 1970-1979

Race and Sex Category of Professionals and Managers	Median Grade Completed and Year										Average Median for Decade
	1970	1971	1972	1973	1974	1975	1976	1977	1978	1979	
Race: Whites	14.9	15.0	15.4	15.5	15.7	15.8	16.0	16.1	16.0	16.1	15.7
Blacks	15.8	15.9	16.0	16.2	16.2	16.4	16.2	16.0	15.6	15.9	16.0
Sex: Males	14.6	14.9	15.3	15.4	15.6	15.9	15.9	16.0	16.0	16.1	15.6
Females	15.5	15.5	15.6	15.9	15.9	16.0	16.0	16.0	15.5	16.1	15.8

Race and Sex Category of Blue-Collar Workers	Median Grade Completed and Year										Average Median for Decade
	1970	1971	1972	1973	1974	1975	1976	1977	1978	1979	
Race: Whites	11.8	12.0	12.1	12.1	12.2	12.2	12.2	12.2	12.2	12.3	12.1
Blacks	10.5	10.8	10.9	11.2	11.6	11.6	11.9	11.7	12.0	12.1	11.4
Sex: Males	11.8	12.0	12.1	12.1	12.2	12.2	12.2	12.2	12.3	12.3	12.1
Females	11.1	11.1	11.2	11.2	11.6	11.8	11.8	11.9	12.1	12.1	11.7

Source: U.S. Labor Department, Handbook of Labor Statistics, Washington D.C.: U.S. Government Printing Office, 1980, pp. 141-146.

Table 5.4
Observed/Expected Ratio of Median School Year Completed for
White Males and for Other Race-Sex Categories for People Employed
as Professionals and Managers and as Blue-Collar Workers,
United States, 1970-1979

Ratio of Grade Completed

Race-Sex Category Ratios for Professionals and Managers	1970	1971	1972	1973	1974	1975	1976	1977	1978	1979	Decade Average
White females: white males	1.05	1.04	1.00	1.03	1.02	1.01	1.01	.99	.98	.99	1.01
Black males: white males	1.00	1.03	1.05	1.05	1.04	1.05	1.01	.96	.94	.96	1.01
Black females: white males	1.12	1.08	1.05	1.06	1.04	1.04	1.02	1.01	1.00	1.00	1.04

Ratio of Grade Completed

Race-Sex Category Ratios for Blue-Collar Workers	1970	1971	1972	1973	1974	1975	1976	1977	1978	1979	Decade Average
White females: white males	.92	.91	.93	.96	.97	.97	.97	.98	.98	.98	.96
Black males: white males	.85	.88	.88	.91	.93	.99	.97	.94	.98	.98	.93
Black females: white males	.97	.97	.96	.97	.98	.99	.97	.98	.98	.98	.98

Source: U.S. Labor Department, Handbook of Labor Statistics, Washington, D.C.: U.S. Government Printing Office, 1980, pp. 141-146.

Wilson claims that the disproportionate number of blacks in low-prestige occupations (compared to whites) is a structural outcome due to their inadequate education. An analysis of ratios in Table 5.4 that treat the white male educational experience as the "ideal type" reveals observed differences less than the ideal type among blue-collar workers of not more than 7 percent for black women, black men, and white women. Among high-status white-collar workers, black women, black men, and white women exceeded by as much as 4 percent the average median grade completed by white males. With the observed educational achievement of the three other race-sex categories deviating not more than 4 percent above and not less than 7 percent below the designated ideal-type median education manifested among white males, one does not find much support for attributing differences in occupational distributions by race to differences in educational attainment between races.

The small difference in educational attainment for populations in lower-status occupational roles favors white males. But the small difference in educational attainment among high-status workers favors black females, not white males. Even among the poor, the miniscule educational lag among blacks and white females (compared to white males) is not substantial and does not adequately account for a difference of 26 percent between the proportion of black males in blue-collar occupations (73 percent) and that of white males (47 percent). Among the affluent, black females who have a slight educational advantage over whites and black males should have a disproportionate share of high-status white-collar jobs, if education is the determining factor in occupation achievement as Wilson suggested. Actually black females are employed as professionals, technical workers, managers, and administrators in the same proportion as black males. And white males, whose educational attainment among high-status employees is slightly less than that of black females, hold down twice the proportion of high-status jobs as black females. Certainly education cannot account for this discrepancy in expected versus actual proportion of high-status jobs held, which favors white males over all other population groups. The data presented in Table 5.4 are evidence in support of the Hauser and Featherman hypothesis that racial discrimination in the process of stratification is primarily socioeconomic.

Discrimination continues by race and by sex in the labor force. Furthermore, these data suggest that discrimination increases as one ascends the stratification hierarchy. Table 5.2 reveals that proportionately black females are overrepresented by 27 percent among blue-collar workers but are underrepresented by 39 percent among professional, technical, managerial, and administrative workers. Further, black females are underrepresented among the high-status workers more than any other race-sex category, despite the fact their average median educational attainment is greater than all others, as revealed in Table

5.3. The data in Table 5.3 suggest that black females, white females, and black males, in that rank order, have to have more education than white males to obtain similar high-status jobs that white males obtain with less education than the other population groups.

There is a hint in the data, but not a conclusive finding, that race may be more significant in consignment to low-status occupations and that sex or gender may be more significant in exclusion from high-status occupations. According to data presented in Table 5.2, three of the race-sex categories are proportionately overrepresented in the low-status blue-collar occupations, and two of these three are of blacks—black males and black females. Also, three race-sex categories are proportionately underrepresented in the high-status white-collar occupations, and two of these three are of females—female blacks and female whites. Further evidence pointing toward this conclusion is the fact that the average overrepresentation of blacks is greater than the underrepresentation of white females among low-status blue-collar workers, and the average underrepresentation of females is greater than the overrepresentation of white males among high-status white-collar workers. Thus, the association among race, gender, and socioeconomic status probably is not the same at both ends of the stratification hierarchy. Erroneous interpretations are likely when conclusions based on an analysis of the association between variables in the lower sector of the stratification hierarchy are projected onto the higher sector, and vice-versa.

This analysis is a warning against the practice of uncritically projecting principles of behavior from situation to situation. Education, for example, may not facilitate access to high-status opportunities the same way that it impedes upward mobility from low-status occupations among racial minorities. Similarly, the association between gender and access to occupations may differ at the top and at the bottom of the stratification hierarchy.

CONCLUSION

Based on the data presented in this analysis, I conclude that there is an association among race, gender, and socioeconomic status but that this association varies among population groups. Further, I conclude that these variables have a different pattern of association at the top and at the bottom of the stratification hierarchy. At the top of the hierarchy, black females, white females, and black males, in that order, need more education than white males to obtain similar high-status jobs that white males obtain with less education. The fact that white males tend to hold a higher proportion of high-status jobs than all other population groups despite their relatively lower average median education among high-status employees casts doubt on the assertion that employment opportunities in the United States are based primarily on merit.

Minority racial status appears to be used both as a reason for consigning people to low-status occupations and for denying them access to high-status occupations. But female gender status, especially among whites, is used more to deny high-status occupational opportunities than for consignment to low-status jobs. Hence race functions in a more pervasive way as a form of oppression, although both gender and race are used to deny high-status opportunities to women and blacks.

This analysis of employment in blue-collar and white-collar occupations confirms the hypothesis that the effects of racial discrimination tend to increase with higher socioeconomic status arrangements in that blacks need more education than do whites to obtain the same high-status jobs that whites obtain with less education. Moreover, this analysis of the blue-collar and white-collar employment experience reveals that discrimination against women also tends to increase as women seek to obtain opportunities toward the top of the stratification hierarchy. They too need more education than males to obtain jobs in which men are employed with less education.

In the light of their double subdominant status, black women experience the most structural discrimination of all population groups. They are consigned to low-status occupations because of their race and denied high-status opportunities because of their gender. To overcome this double jeopardy, they require more education than all other population groups to experience parity with them.

Black men also are consigned to the low-status opportunities and excluded from the high. They are consigned to low-status blue-collar occupations more than any other race-sex category and excluded from high-status, white-collar occupations more than any other group except black women, with whom they share the common destiny of most excluded from opportunities at the upper end of the stratification hierarchy. While the consignment of black men to low-status occupations is a structural effect in a racist society, the exclusion of black men from high-status opportunities is not a structural effect in a sexist society that favors males. It is a contradiction in the application of sexist norms. This means that the way black men overcome their oppression may differ from the way black women cope because of differences in their circumstances.

White women who are underrepresented among workers in blue-collar occupations probably are less consigned to low-status jobs than black women and black men because of their dominant racial status in a racist society. Thus they benefit in avoiding some low-status adversities because of the application of racist norms but suffer exclusion from some high-status opportunities because of their sex category in a sexist society. White women suffer from the application of sexist norms and benefit from the application of racist norms. White women experience structural norms that both support and constrain them. Thus, their adaptations and coping skills necessarily differ from those of black women and black men, whose normative condition they do not fully share.

White men have double opportunities reinforced by racist norms that favor whites and sexist norms that favor males. Their opportunities are structurally sanctioned by social norms. Thus, they disproportionately participate in high-status opportunities even when they are not the most meritorious. Dismantling the unjust normative system is the primary route available to white males for coping with the sexist and racist benefits they unfairly enjoy. Until this is done, one must conclude that white men benefit more from structural oppression than does any other population group.

This analysis of the alternative forms of coping and adapting required of different race-sex categories to overcome adversity and injustice indicates the error of projecting solutions appropriate for one situation to another when circumstances and conditions are population specific.

REFERENCES

Hauser, Robert M., and David L. Featherman. 1977. *The Process of Stratification.* New York: Academic Books.

Miller, Herman. 1965. "The Dimension of Poverty." In Ben E. Seligman, ed., *Poverty as a Public Issue.* New York: Free Press.

Seligman, Ben E., ed. 1965. *Poverty as a Public Issue.* New York: Free Press.

U.S. Department of Labor. 1980. *Handbook of Labor Statistics.* Washington, D.C.: U.S. Government Printing Office.

Willie, Charles Vert. 1979. *The Caste and Class Controversy.* Bayside, N.Y.: General Hall.

Wilson, William. 1978. *The Declining Significance of Race.* Chicago: University of Chicago Press.

6
Dominant and Subdominant Populations: Toward a Theory of Complementarity

Several years ago, Daniel Patrick Moynihan asserted, "It is clearly a disadvantage for a minority group to be operating on one principle, while the great majority of the population, and the one with the most advantages to begin with, is operating on another" (Moynihan 1965:29). This statement suggests that minorities should be remade in the image of values of the majority (Willie 1977:28) to participate fully in the society and its opportunity structure. It was Moynihan's belief that progress was retarded for those who are "out of line with the rest of American society" (Moynihan 1965:29). This view, in part, was articulated earlier by E. Franklin Frazier. In his polemical essays "The Failure of the Negro Intellectual" and "Inferiority Complex and Quest for Status," Frazier described middle-class or affluent blacks as "outsiders in American life" who create "a world of make-believe" (Frazier 1968:225, 270). This, in Frazier's opinion, accounted for their alleged "failure," especially that of black intellectuals.

This chapter challenges the view that minorities, including those who are affluent, working class, and poor, are outsiders in the United States and that their full participation in society requires adoption of cultural patterns of the majority. Indeed a thesis of this chapter is that it is dysfunctional in society for the minority to imitate the majority and that an effectively functioning society encourages minority and majority groups to interact as complementary populations, with one group doing for the other what the other group cannot do for itself. This thesis also is in accord with the traditional wisdom wherein one is admonished to recognize "varieties of gifts" in society for the benefit of all (Corinthians 12).

Based on a review of the literature of white family life and my study of eighteen black families reported in *A New Look at Black Families*, I concluded, "Black families and white families in the United States share a common core of values," "they adapt to the society and its values in different ways, largely because of their dominant and subdominant situations," and finally, "the life-style of one social class cannot be understood apart from that of other social classes" (Willie 1981:220). These findings led me to develop a hypothesis that white families and black families, representatives of dominant and subdominant cultural groups, respectively, are complementary. If this is so, they necessarily adapt differently to common experiences. Since all knowledge is partial, dominant and subdominant groups teach each other by sharing their different understandings of what is appropriate and inappropriate; subdominants contribute to the incomplete knowledge of dominants and dominants add to the partial knowledge of subdominants. Contrary to Moynihan's assertion, it makes sense for blacks and whites in a common society to operate on different sets of principles if this hypothesis is confirmed.

Principles have to do with exploration, the discovery of limits and directions (Brumbaugh 1985:64). The limits and directions for dominants and subdominants differ because of their social locations and existential histories connected with such locations. For example, cooperative effort for mutual benefit requires different actions by dominants and by subdominants. Dominants who command disproportionate power and resources in social organization are generous and give more than required when they are cooperative. But subdominants who have less power and resources than others are magnanimous when they cooperate for mutual benefit—thereby taking less than entitled. In an effectively functioning society of mutuality, magnanimous behavior does not penalize subdominants because dominants recognize that a society of "genuine equality of opportunity . . . must give more attention to those with fewer . . . assets and to those . . . [in] the less favorable social positions" (Rawls 1971:100).

Societies fulfill this requirement because of the difference principle, which in effect is a social contract that "regard[s] the distribution of . . . talents as a common asset" for mutual benefit (Rawls 1971:101). Recognizing the reality of differences, including disparity in access to and distribution of resources within society, W. Arthur Lewis suggests that a sensible economic plan, for example, invests the nation's limited resources in those areas with the best productive prospects. This can be done, he states, with a minimum of resistances from those in areas with fewer resources if all citizens have a right to participate equally in any part of the country and "if some of the wealth produced in the richer areas [is used] to finance improved facilities in the poor areas" (Lewis 1966:69). Robert Merton deals with this principle in a succinct observation: there is an "obligation for generosity of behavior by those enjoying rank and power" (Merton 1976:80).

The principle of complementarity has to do with applied metaphysics —that is, how to implement the principle of difference in a mutually satisfying way for different population groups. Because of the under-developed nature of applied social science in the United States (Brumbaugh 1984:67), there is little understanding of how functional differences among dominant and subdominant groups may function for the benefit of the whole. Policy makers such as Moynihan, because of their limited comprehension of applied metaphysics, are fearful of differences and the conflict they may generate. With a better knowledge of the principle of complementarity, how it operates, and circumstances resulting therefrom, policy makers may realize that the principle of difference can be the basis for cooperation as well as conflict and competition. If Moynihan had had a fuller understanding of the way that black populations and white populations in the United States complement each other, he may have been less inclined to use the way of life of whites as an ideal type for all and to predict negative outcomes for blacks when they do not act as whites do. Actually the total society benefits when blacks act the way that subdominants should act and when whites act the way that dominants should act.

Dominant status is not an intrinsic property of the white population, and subdominant status is not an intrinsic property of the black population. Whites, blacks, or other population groups are dominants when their members collectively control disproportionate resources, have the authority to choose action strategies, and have the organizational capacity to commit resources for the implementation of such choices. Thus the indicated behavior of a particular population group in social organization is not so much a function of its racial or ethnic heritage as it is a function of its dominant or subdominant status in the community's power structure. Any population may function as a dominant or subdominant power group. This is a variable function that depends on situations and circumstances.

It is important to determine whether a group is dominant or subdominant "because these two categories have different responsibilities in power relationships. Subdominants cannot do for dominants what dominants must do for themselves. And dominants cannot do for subdominants what subdominants must do for themselves" (Willie 1983:240). Each group, however, can do for the other what the other cannot do for itself. To illustrate, dominants by precept and example can teach subdominants how to be generous; similarly, subdominants can teach dominants how to be magnanimous. Both magnanimity and generosity are necessary in an effectively functioning society.

That the orientations and definitions of the dominant and subdominant racial populations in the United States complement each other is demonstrated by findings of my recent study of alternative definitions of excellence among professional educators offered by black and by white humanists and social scientists (Willie 1986). In this study, I asked members of the governing councils of national professional associations to nominate the most outstanding black scholar in their respective fields, as mentioned in Chapter 4. The nominations were submitted to a random sample of black and of white senior members for ranking. Data reported are the reasons given by 222 white and 152 black professionals for ranking a particular scholar as the most outstanding.

These rankings indicated that black scholars and white scholars share a common core of values and some that are different. Blacks and whites agreed that research, writing, and publishing (generically called scholarship) are the most important components of outstanding professional status. After agreement on the most important characteristic, unanimity between the races disappeared. Following scholarship, blacks listed competence and public service; professional association activity and commitment to the black community tied for fourth place in their hierarchy of components that characterize outstanding professionals in the humanities and social sciences. In addition to scholarship, whites listed, in the order given, professional association activity, professional reputation, and public service as the most important characteristics of an outstanding black professional educator (Willie 1986:chap. 1).

In this list of six important characteristics of excellent professional black educators, blacks and whites agreed with only minor differences in the rank ordering of scholarship, professional association activity, and public service. They disagreed on the relative importance of competence, professional reputation, and commitment to the black community. In analyzing these differences by race, I concluded that

competence and professional reputation are different indicators of the same phenomenon. Blacks prefer to assess intelligence . . . directly as a personal attribute which they call *competence*. Whites prefer to assess [intelligence] indirectly as a reflection of *reputation*. If we assume that competence and professional reputation are merely two different indicators of intelligence, . . . then the major difference between the races in their hierarchies of criteria is the inclusion [by blacks] of commitment to the black community. . . .

According to the hierarchy of values expressed by blacks in our study, no one who is callous about oppression, indifferent or uncommitted to the people who experience it, can be considered an outstanding scholar in the humanities and social sciences. . . . Blacks have added an ethical requirement of concern for the . . . oppressed . . . for those [whom they classify] outstanding. (Willie 1986:chap. 1)

This concern was not expressed by whites in their list of characteristics.

The absence of concern by whites about a target population that should benefit from scholarly endeavors constitutes a fundamental difference between the races in their definition of outstanding professional status. Clearly blacks are concerned about applied social science. What one knows is an important component of scholarly excellence, which both racial populations recognize. However, blacks who are subdominant in the American power structure label members of their group outstanding only if they also are committed to uplifting the subdominant population. This difference in the definition of outstanding professional status by black scholars and white scholars is fundamdental, not frivolous. The subdominants in the study used indicators of individual enhancement, as did the dominants in identifying top scholars. The subdominants also included an indicator of group advancement (commitment to the black community).

On the basis of this analysis, one can say that subdominants keep applied social science on the agendas of their disciplines. It should be self-evident that both discovery and application of knowledge are important problems to solve in social science. Commenting on the pressing need for solving the problem of application of knowledge, philosopher Robert Brumbaugh asserted that "we have no applied metaphysics today . . . the translation from principle to practice is unsystematic, a diffusion by accident; there is no disciplined attention (Brumbaugh 1984:63).

So that the full range of problems of a discipline is kept before its professional members, the participation of dominants and subdominants is essential. The frame of reference of dominants cannot and should not be substituted for that of subdominants. The frames of references of dominants and subdominants in a discipline—one emphasizing discovery of knowledge and the other emphasizing application of knowledge—are complementary.

Our difficulty in acknowledging the principle of complementarity and the significance of knowledge application in social science is due largely to our difficulty in acknowledging the principle of difference that pertains to knowledge and discovery in social science. There is a tendency on the part of dominants in the society at large as well as in the disciplines to deny the existence of the principle of difference. This denial clearly was manifested in Moynihan's assertion mentioned at the beginning of this chapter. It also was mentioned by some white participants in my study of outstanding black scholars. Comments of a few whites who declined to rank the panel of black scholars manifested the denial syndrome. One said, "The study is racist since scholarly excellence is the same for all racial groups." The covering letter requesting participation in the study asserted that the life history of the ranking black scholar obviously would be useful as a role model. Questioning this assertion, a member of the dominant group said, "I don't agree that your proposed life-history will be of obvious value; why should it be of any more value than role-models such as Curie, Galileo, or Archimedes?" On and on the practice of denial of the principle of difference goes from Daniel Patrick Moynihan in his report on the black family to the white participants in my study of outstanding black scholars.

We must embrace the principle of difference before we can understand the principle of complementarity. Our social science disciplines are a long way from doing this because the dominants who are afflicted the most by the denial syndrome have the power to implement in the discipline their views which are partial and incomplete.

REFERENCES

Brumbaugh, Robert S. 1984. *Unreality and Time*. Albany: State University of New York Press.
Frazier, E. Franklin. 1968. "The Failure of the Negro Intellectual" and "Inferiority Complex and Quest for Status." In G. Franklin Edwards, ed., *Franklin Frazier on Race Relations*. Chicago: University of Chicago Press.
Lewis, W. Arthur. 1966. *Development Planning*. London: George Allen.
Merton, Robert K. 1976. *Sociological Ambivalence and Other Essays*. New York: Free Press.
Moynihan, Daniel P. 1965. *The Negro Family, The Case for National Action*. Washington, D.C.: U.S. Government Printing Office.
Rawls, John. 1971. *A Theory of Justice*. Cambridge, Mass.: Harvard University Press.
Willie, Charles Vert. 1977. *Black/Brown/White Relations*. New Brunswick, N.J.: Transaction Books.
_____. 1981. *A New Look at Black Families*. Bayside, N.Y.: General Hall.
_____. 1983. *Race, Ethnicity, and Socioeconomic Status*. Bayside, N.Y.: General Hall.
_____. 1986. *Five Black Scholars*. Cambridge, Mass.: Abt Books.

Part III

EFFECTIVE SCHOOLING

7
Leadership Development Programs

Innovative social programs seldom travel straight paths if appropriate arrangements are not made to assess their cultural, economic, social, and political impact during the planning stage, according to Weiss and Fuller (1983:189). The evaluation study reported here suffered because of such planning defects. Formal assessment of outcome was not required of most of the leadership development programs for minorities when these programs were launched or funded by the Rockefeller Foundation largely during the closing years of the 1960s and throughout the 1970s. When this evaluation was attempted nearly a decade after some of the programs had begun, input, process, and outcome had to be inferred from reports, records, and other administrative data.

Since these are the only data available for a post hoc analysis of most community action programs, this study explores whether these data are of any value in evaluation. The Foundation wanted answers to general questions: What were the goals of the leadership development programs? Were these goals achieved? What were the consequences of the programs, both anticipated and unanticipated? In addition to answering these, the study investigated questions having to do with program effectiveness and alternative methods of operation. Answers were sought for specific questions pertaining to social organization and social control: Are leadership development programs for minorities more effective when operated by a minority-group-controlled agency rather than a majority-group-controlled agency? Are such programs that emphasize precept and example as the main instructional strategy more effective than those that require formal education? Are programs in formal education for leadership development that are sponsored by an educational institution more effective than those operated by a voluntary association?

The purpose of the leadership development programs was to bring more minorities into the mainstream of U.S. society and its political, economic, and educational institutions. By examining input, process, and outcome variables for selected programs on a retrospective basis, tentative answers may be provided and hypotheses formulated for further study. No definitive conclusions are possible because of the kinds of data available for analysis.

That leadership development programs for minorities are seldom evaluated could be classified as a benign form of racism. Foundations that launch such programs without examining their effect telegraph a message to the public that effort is more important than the outcome when dealing with minorities. This evaluation, although difficult because it was not planned when the leadership development programs were launched, attempts to send a different message—that knowledge of success or failure of programs for minorities is as important as knowledge of success or failure of programs for the majority.

A multimillion dollar leadership development program launched by another foundation during the same period covered in this study awarded fellowships to hundreds of individuals without any "firm criteria for selecting fellows" and then declared eight years after its beginning that the value of the program had been realized, although it "lack[ed] specific aims and results," according to an independent observer (Nevin 1981:8, 10). Minorities deserve a better assessment of the outcome of programs intended for their benefit. This study is an attempt to reach that goal. The evaluation of programs for the advancement of minorities should receive serious attention.

DATA AND METHOD

The various programs studied are not offered as representative of all leadership development programs. Chombart deLauwe indicates the value of studying cultural models by way of field surveys, documentary research, and analysis of content (1964a:151). He states that these can be observed of individuals or of groups in natural settings and that "large-scale samplings are not always the most important part of sociological studies in the urban milieux" (1964b:55). In fact, he states that a leading place should be given to comparative studies on small samples "without representativeness being necessarily aimed at" (p. 65).

This is precisely the approach taken in this evaluation study. Ad hoc groups were selected for systematic analysis. Two human resources fellowship programs that trained minorities for administrative roles in public-service agencies were examined. One program was administered by the Rockefeller Foundation, and the other by a minority-group-controlled voluntary agency that specialized in public policy research. These two programs were compared to determine differences, if any, in effectiveness when operated by majority-group and by minority-group organizations.

These two programs that used precept and example (or apprenticeship) as the main instructional strategy were combined as a single program for the purpose of analysis and then compared with another human services program that had a formal education component. This comparison determined whether for minorities apprenticeship programs were more effective than those that required formal education and awarded academic degrees. The program that had a formal education component then was compared with another that awarded an academic degree. However, the second of these programs was administered by an institution of higher education, whereas the first was not, although it contracted with a university for the educational component. The goal here was to determine differences in effect, if any, for leadership development programs with educational components that are controlled by educational and noneducational institutions. In summary, four leadership development programs were selected for detailed analysis of input, process, and outcome factors.

FINDINGS

The Human Resources Fellowship Program, initiated in 1972 and operated for three years by the Foundation (identified in this analysis as a majority-controlled organization), was turned over to a predominantly black-policy-studies private association in Wahington, D.C., in 1976 and continued for another three years until 1979. The goal of this program was the development of a cadre of qualified and experienced minority administrators capable of assuming responsible positions in the human resources delivery system after completing one-year internships.

During the three years that the program was administered by the majority-controlled organization, an average of three interns per year were placed, for a total of nine. They were recruited through an extensive information-dissemination network from various national minority-group organizations and some local governmental agencies. Admission to the program followed an elaborate screening process that included the compilation of information on each applicant by the staff, nominations by two consultants—one an education administrator and the other a human services administrator—who based their decisions on the staff information, and, finally, interviews of the nominees by the staff. Before entering the program, the fellows who had completed college were employed in a variety of entry-level positions (such as assistant director or coordinator) in local government and in other agencies. The interns were said to be highly motivated. Interns were placed largely in federal government, but not with highest-level decision makers. The majority-controlled organization did not provide postinternship placement assistance for the minorities. Interns who found jobs after the year of apprenticeship returned to positions similar to those they had before entering the program. They were not promoted to jobs with line authority. The annual cost per intern for the nine appointed during the three-year period was approximately $33,333.

When the Human Resources Fellowship Program for minorities was transferred to a minority-controlled organization, an average of six interns per year were accommodated for a total of seventeen during the three-year period. The minority-controlled organization recruited individuals described by the staff as middle-level administrators with master's degrees. Recruitment was nationwide, but information dissemination was not extensive and neither was the selection process, which was done with in-house staff only. A graduate degree was used as an indicator of previous achievement by potential participants. Their job titles were assistant analyst, assistant director, and other positions of similar rank. Most were apprenticed to federal officials who assumed middle-level administrative responsibilities in governmental bureaucracies. The participants said the work they performed as apprentices was not unlike what they did before entering the program. Most of the interns remained in Washington after their apprenticeships ended but had difficulty finding jobs they believed were appropriate to their education and experience. They wished that postinternship placement assistance had been given. The average annual cost per intern for the program administered by the minority-controlled organization was $29,000.

The major difference between programs administered by the majority-controlled and minority-controlled organizations was in the number of people served. During the same time period, the minority-controlled organization accommodated almost twice as many participants as its comparison program and at a slightly lower cost per person. Another difference was the reported level of motivation and the actual education of participants in the two programs. Because of the elaborate selection process of the majority-controlled organization, the few minorities who survived the screening appeared to be more highly motivated than participants in the other program. But those selected by the minority-controlled organization were more highly educated. This difference may reflect a significant variation in definition of cause of discrimination by the two groups.

Dominants tend to attribute failure and hardship to deficiency within the individual, whereas subdominants tend to attribute the failure and hardship to defects in the social system (Willie 1983:205). Thus, the majority-group-sponsored program recruited individuals made of "sterner stuff" who could transform difficulties into new opportunities, while the minority-group-sponsored program recruited overqualified individuals who because of their superior education might transcend difficulties in pursuit of new opportunities. This orientation of racial minorities is not different from that of other groups who are subdominant in the power structure and are discriminated against. For example, a female surgeon advises: "Always do your best. Especially as a woman. You have to try harder. You can't be satisfied with being as good as the men. You have to be better. Otherwise they won't respect you" (Morgan 1980:161).

Clearly, these human-resource leadership development programs erred in assuming that qualified minorities would be welcomed into the mainstream of society after receiving appropriate training. The decision not to follow through in the placement of participants harmed participants in both programs. Minorities and other subdominant populations need intercessors and advocates as well as groups that support and sustain them (Willie 1983:124-129). They need someone to monitor the systems to determine whether they are making a proper response and following through in an equitable way.

Although neither program had a notable short-range effect on career mobility for minorities, both programs provided new experiences for their participants and enabled them to hold their own at the level at which they were functioning before the internships. Our investigation could not assess long-range effects. While there was not an immediate leap forward into positions of line authority, there was no backsliding either.

The fact that minority-controlled and majority-controlled programs had more or less the same outcomes suggests that neither internship program dealt with what apparently is a primary blockage in employment opportunities for subdominants—a malfunctioning placement process.

The combined Human Resources Fellowship Program represented a six-year effort in behalf of twenty-six minority individuals. Because the outcome was similar in both programs, it is fair to join them as one for further analysis to determine differences, if any, in the effect of a training program that relied entirely on an apprenticeship strategy and one that involved formal training as well as precept and example. The apprenticeship program was described earlier. It will be compared with a National Fellows in Education and Legislation Program that was sponsored by a Hispanic association based in New York City. The comparison program operated during a four-year period from 1975 to 1979 and provided on-the-job training and academic courses leading to a degree in urban education. This human services training program included an educational component because of the belief by its sponsoring organization that academic credentials play an important role in career development, especially for minorities.

This Hispanic-sponsored human services program served eighteen—four to five persons each year. Participants were recruited and admitted to the program by the sponsoring organization. Minimum qualifications were a bachelor's degree, two years of work experience in administration, and a desire to become a policy maker. Most of the participants were interested in becoming urban policy specialists capable of administering a range of human services in an urban setting, including, but not limited to, education. In accordance with the terms of a contract with a private university, the participants in the Hispanic-controlled program studied during the summer session before their internship and the summer after. The summer session courses were in urban research, urban problems, conflict resolution, mediation, and supervision. By enrolling in six courses each summer, a field-study course and one other course during the regular school year, thirty academic credits could be earned. This was enough for a master's degree in urban education. Seventeen of the eighteen participants in the program received graduate degrees. Meanwhile during the fall, winter, and spring, they served as interns in a number of agencies; several were placed in Washington, D.C.

The jobs that the participants received after completing the fifteen-month program had to do with bilingual education or were related directly to the Hispanic community in some other way. Only three of the eighteen participants found employment with the federal government after completing the program. The academic study apparently awakened a latent interest in three or four participants who enrolled in doctoral degree programs after receiving their master's degrees. Immediately after the program ended, most participants found jobs as assistant deans, coordinators, assistant directors, technical assistants, program directors, and teachers. They left such jobs as planners, social workers, coordinators, research associates, assistant directors, program directors, and teacher-interns when they came into the program. It is fair to say that the kinds of jobs most of the participants received immediately after participating in the program of study and on-the-job training were not much different from the kinds of jobs they had before the program began. Again the time frame in which the evaluation was made does not permit an assessment of the long-range effects.

It is significant, however, that a human services training program that included an educational component stimulated approximately one-fourth of the participants who received an academic degree to continue studying for a second postgraduate degree. This proportion represents a critical mass that is worthy of noting. None of the training programs that used precept and example as the principal instructional technique stimulated an immediate desire for further study in the participants, even though some of them already had master's degrees.

When this Hispanic-controlled human services training program began, little attention was given to the matter of placement. After the third year, the program staff recognized the essential role of placement and launched a job referral service during the fourth and final year. The sponsoring organization found such a service especially helpful in assisting graduates of the program to obtain employment in federal agencies. Before the job referral service began, most of the Hispanic graduates of the fifteen-month program found employment elsewhere in the nation, despite the fact that many held internships in Washington, D.C.

Comparing the Hispanic-sponsored leadership development program that involved formal study and apprenticeship with the Human Resources Fellowship Program that was limited to apprenticeship only, I conclude that the program of study is a useful addition. Moreover, it is no more expensive than a straight internship. The average annual cost per intern in the Hispanic-sponsored program was $24,083—a sum less than both the apprenticeship programs discussed earlier. In addition to receiving on-the-job training and an academic degree, a substantial number of participants in the university-connected program were encouraged to continue studying for doctoral degrees. This is a significant outcome if subdominants indeed must be overqualified to be respected and to obtain the same kinds of jobs that some dominants get with lesser qualifications, as indicated in Chapter 5.

Finally, I examined the issue of whether a human services training program for minorities that involves formal study and learning by precept and example is more effective when operated by an educational institution than when operated by a voluntary association such as the Hispanic group already mentioned. The university-controlled program for minorities was located in a public institution of higher education in New York State. This program, totally controlled by the university, served twenty-three participants during a seven-year period—three to four students a year. The annual cost per participant was $24,519—about the same as that for the Hispanic-controlled program that had only a contractual relationship with a university. The major difference between the university-controlled program and others was the length of time required to complete it: three years. The university-controlled program obviously was an educational program primarily with an apprenticeship component.

During the regular school year, students enrolled in college courses and functioned as regular members of the campus community. College study was supplemented with internships during two consecutive summers. The state university designed the program to train minority-group students for careers in the public sector.

High-aptitude but low-performing students were recruited from central-city community colleges. During the first year on campus, which was the third year of college study for the community college graduates, a massive support system was provided. The unique tutorials and other special arrangements were designed to help the students through what the college called an "accelerated" period of study. The tutorial assistance was particularly helpful for students with an aptitude for but low performance in mathematics. Although the curriculum emphasized difficult subjects, such as quantitative methods of analysis, economic theory, and the management of resources in urban settings, most students were able to move into the mainstream of college work in the second year of their matriculation.

The enrollment of minority students in this special program at the state university continued into a third year. Although they will have already completed four years of college, including two years at the university and two years at the community college, degrees were not awarded until the fifth year was finished. The final year of the program integrated experiences from study and preceptorships by way of a series of case studies about decision-making problems in government. Minority students who completed the three-year special program were awarded a combined bachelor's and master's degree in urban and policy sciences.

The state university went to work on behalf of the minority students in the special program to help them find suitable jobs. All students were placed in good entry-level jobs that offered opportunities for advancement. The graduates of this combination education-preceptorship program obtained such jobs as research associate, program analyst, and budget analyst in federal, state, and local government. Three of the twenty-three immediately continued their education, enrolling in professional or academic programs of study for the doctoral degree.

By being fully in control, the state university was able to design a comprehensive educational program with an apprenticeship component. The university recruited the participants, designed the curriculum, provided tutorial help when needed, found suitable internships for the summer, and assisted the graduates in finding jobs after they received two degrees certifying their completion of a demanding course of study. In summary, the university-controlled program was committed to its students from recruitment through instruction and after graduation. Such support, endorsement, and intercession are valuable experiences for members of subdominant populations. Apparently institutions of higher education are able to negotiate with other institutions on behalf of all students —including minority students—better than free-standing associations such as those that serve minority constituents.

CONCLUSIONS

The overall conclusion is that the most effective leadership-development program for minorities that offers the greatest possibility of bringing members into the mainstream is an educational program with an apprenticeship component that equips participants with both experience and an academic degree. Such a program is best implemented under the control and auspices of an institution of higher education that provides comprehensive educational services, including recruitment, financial aid, curriculum development, supportive services, and placement. Of lesser importance in equipping minorities for the mainstream, in descending order, are apprenticeship programs with education components, and apprenticeship programs that rely solely on precept and example as a learning strategy.

An unanticipated finding of this study is the significance of placement as an educational service. It is essential and is found in all good leadership development programs for minorities and other subdominant populations. Without a good placement program, the training in schools of good learning may be of limited benefit. Even after receiving a good education, minorities need advocates and intercessors who have sufficient institutional strength to contend against resisting systems, to persevere, and to overcome so that justice may be done.

REFERENCES

Chombart deLauwe, P. H. 1964a. "Field and Case Studies." In P. Hauser, ed., *Handbook for Social Research in Urban Areas*, pp. 55-72. Brussels: UNESCO.
_____. 1964b. "Social Organization in an Urban Milieu." In P. Hauser, ed., *Handbook for Social Research in Urban Areas*, pp. 140-58. Brussels: UNESCO.
Morgan, E. 1981. *The Making of a Woman Surgeon*. New York: Putnam.
Nevin, D. 1981. *Left-Handed Fastballers, Scouting and Training America's Grass-Roots Leaders, 1966-1977*. New York: Ford Foundation.
Weiss, C. H., and R. D. Fuller. 1983. "On Evaluating Development Assistance Projects." *Evaluation Review* 7:175-90.
Willie, Charles Vert. 1983. *Race, Ethnicity, and Socioeconomic Status*. Bayside, N.Y.: General Hall.

8
Educating Liberation Leaders

At the conclusion of chapter 6, entitled "Of the Training of Black Men," in his book, *The Souls of Black Folk,* W. E. B. Du Bois gave his version of what a classical education could do for a black person, for a white person, for any other person. In Du Bois' view, learning was wedded to truth, and truth dwelled above the mass, the cloistered, the commonplace. In some of the best of his lyrical phrases, Du Bois—the black intellectual—concluded the chapter thus:

I sit with Shakespeare and he winces not. Across the color line I move arm and arm with Balzac and Dumas, where smiling men and welcoming women glide in gilded halls. From out of the caves of evening that swing between the strong-limbed earth and the tracery of the stars, I summon Aristotle and Aurelius and what soul I will, and they come graciously with no scorn nor condescension. So, wed with Truth, I dwell above the Veil. Is this the life you grudge us, O knightly America? Is this the life you long to change into the dull red hideousness of Georgia? (1903a:87)

This was Du Bois' version of what an education could do, what an education should do for those who diligently pursue it. Education, as he understood it, was one way of communing across the color line. Education was one way of escaping the "dull red hideousness of Georgia" or the Black Belt poverty of Alabama. The irony is that the dull red hideousness of Georgia produced one of the most magnificent liberation leaders the world has ever known—Martin Luther King, Jr.

Although emerging from Georgia, Martin Luther King, Jr., received a classical and career-oriented education. He finished a course of study in the common schools of Atlanta, Georgia, and began higher education there. He graduated from Morehouse, a men's liberal arts college in Atlanta, Georgia; Crozier Theological Seminary in Chester, Pennsylvania; and the graduate school of Boston University in Massachusetts. He earned a doctor of philosophy degree. He did all of these things, but as an educated person he did not escape. King's first job was in the Black Belt region of Alabama, where he was minister to a church congregation in Montgomery. Then he moved on to the red hills of Atlanta, Georgia.

Martin Luther King, Jr., was not above the veil; he was not beyond the commonplace. He lost his life in Memphis, where he had gone to demonstrate for better working conditions in behalf of men who collect garbage. King recalled the sayings of Aristotle and Aurelius in his speeches, as Du Bois said an educated person should, but Martin Luther King, Jr., could do even more. He knew how to share in the joys and sorrows of the meek, humble, and poor. It was because of his involvement in Alabama, not despite it, that he became a national leader. It was because of his origin on "Sweet Auburn Avenue" in Georgia, not despite it, that he rose to international acclaim.

King was exceptional. Du Bois said that "the Negro race, like all other races, is going to be saved by its exceptional people" (1903b:228). Du Bois' concept linked leadership with education in a hierarchy in which there were teachers and teachers of teachers. His hierarchy did not include the suffering servant as leader, which King was. Thus, Du Bois' concept of leadership for minorities probably was partial and incomplete, as the lives of King, Gandhi, and Moses reveal.

The Du Bois theory linked education directly to leadership and did not consider intervening variables that are essential in effective leadership. Because the ideas of Du Bois underlie many contemporary approaches to the development of black leadership, it is time to reexamine the premises on which some practices are based, in the light of an analysis of the lives of genuine liberation leaders.

Du Bois believed that education cultivates a sane self-interest that seeks to find the rights of all as a way of avoiding national decadence. He rejected the notion of education as an embellishment. Du Bois believed that learnings in the common school—or what he called the "outer courts of knowledge"—should be available to all. But he accepted the idea that higher education should be available to a selective few, who by reason of "deftness and aim, talent and character" (rather than by birth or wealth) are able to comprehend "its mystery of truth [that] is revealed" (Du Bois 1903a:75-76).

Clearly there was a hierarchical pattern in leadership in Du Bois' thinking, so much so that he would call the teachers, and the teachers of teachers, the "talented tenth." He described them as the "men and women of knowledge and culture and technical skill who understand modern civilization . . . and have the training and aptitude to impart it to [those] under them." According to Du Bois, the talented tenth should be made leaders of thought and missionaries of culture among black people (Du Bois 1903b:228).

History has revealed that many good leaders are well-educated people. But well-educated people are not always good leaders. Du Bois' theory directly linking education and leadership acknowledges the former but is silent about the latter principle. The assertion of a direct linkage between education and leadership, then, was the error in his theory; for liberation leadership to develop, something in addition to education is needed.

One source of error in Du Bois' theory of leadership development is his assumption that hierarchy is the natural order of social relationships and that those above should give direction to those below. Probably this assumption was influenced by the Harvard heritage of Du Bois. In essence, Du Bois was an elitist. "Progress in human affairs," he said, "is more often a pull than a push, a surging forward of the exceptional man, and the lifting of his duller brethren slowly and painfully to his vantage ground. . . . Thus it was no accident that gave birth to universities centuries before the common schools, that made fair Harvard the first flower of our wilderness." It was his opinion that black colleges had an identical aim as Harvard during the early years of their existence. They wanted, above all, to furnish the black world with "adequate standards of human culture and lofty ideals of life." Of the northerners who came to the South to educate blacks, he said, "The colleges they founded were social settlements; home where the best of the sons of the freedmen came in close and sympathetic touch with the best traditions of New England" (Du Bois 1903a:78, 80, 82).

There are other principles about leadership that mention the concept of hierarchy but that reverse what Du Bois believed was a natural order of social relations. The other concepts of hierarchy and leadership are these: the greatest of all is first the servant of all, and the meek shall have the earth for their possession. Du Bois' theory did not embrace these principles.

To examine Du Bois' theory linking education directly to leadership development, I used the inductive method of analysis and looked at three liberation leaders. Historians agree that three of the greatest freedom fighters for oppressed people who accomplished their goal of deliverance from bondage were Moses, Mohandas K. Gandhi, and Martin Luther King, Jr. The lives of these leaders are examined separately and comparatively to determine their common characteristics and experiences and those that are unique.

The Moses saga tells us that he was born of Hebrew parents who had been poor tribal herders but at that time occupied the land of Goshen to the east of the Nile delta in Egypt. These people were fruitful and multiplied. Pharaoh feared the expanding population of the Hebrew people and thought that in the event of war, they would side with the invaders, and therefore he instituted a population control policy that required midwives to kill all Hebrew male infants. A further order came down on how to accomplish this goal: every live-born Hebrew boy was to be drowned. Moses' mother was able to hide him. She determined that the best hiding place was a clay-lined watertight basket in which she laid the baby among the reeds of the river bank. Meanwhile the Israelis were enslaved by Pharaoh and ordered to help in erecting buildings and monuments.

Pharaoh's daughter, who was sterile and without a child, participated in a fertility rite, periodically washing herself with milk and dousing herself with water. While at the river to partake in this rite one day, a floating basket came her way and was drawn form the river waters. She and her household agreed that the river had responded to the ritual and had sent her a baby.

She named the child Moses, adopting him as her own, and unknowingly retained the Hebrew child's natural mother as nursemaid. Moses grew up as if he were a prince. The royal household he lived in was magnificent and full of precious items. He shared living quarters with a priest and a tutor. He was taught hieroglyphic symbols and how to use weapons. He was a good, bright student. His growing up was sheltered, but he learned about anatomy and medicine. When he traveled, he carried documents with Pharaoh's seal on them (Keneally 1975:7-41). Moses was well educated, but he was not a liberation leader in his young adult years.

Moses did not become a liberation leader until he had fled from Egypt and the life of privilege in Pharaoh's household. As a free person standing near the mountain top in the serene desert, he decided that he would confront injustice in a nonviolent way, that he would forsake the safety and serenity of the desert life, that he would not make peace with oppression and injustice, and that he would return to the household of Pharaoh not to reclaim his royal rank (as he had been invited to do by the new Pharaoh, who had been his boyhood friend) but to denounce slavery and demand its end. Moses became a liberation leader, in the words of Mays, when he became sensitive to the wrongs, the sufferings, and the injustices of society and was willing to accept responsibility for correcting those ills. (Willie and Edmonds 1978:13)

Moses' education was important, but it was linked to leadership only after his double choice—a renouncement of vainglory and a commitment to make no peace with oppression. Without having made these choices, Moses' education would not have resulted in leadership for liberation. The link between leadership and education is not natural or inevitable. It must be cultivated and mediated by personal choices.

Moses made good use of his education in his negotiation sessions with

Pharaoh and his court. He knew their prides, fears, and prejudices because he had lived as a member of the royal court. He had knowledge of the magic and the science of Pharaoh's physicians. He knew of the recurring events in Egyptian culture and the seasons of change and environmental developments associated with them. He used his knowledge of these to generate within the court of Pharaoh a fear of ominous things to come. Sociologist Earl Bell once said that one can exercise a measure of control over any people if one knows their prides, fears, and prejudices and understands how to deal with them. Moses had such knowledge and understanding.

Moreover, Moses understood both Egyptian and Israeli ways of life. He had been socialized in these double cultures. Issuing forth from two heritages, he qualified as a genuine marginal person—one exposed to two worlds who became wiser because of these dual experiences. Moses, a well-educated marginal person who renounced vain glory and committed his life to the achievement of social justice, became a liberation leader of his people, leading them away from slavery and out of captivity. And "the [Jewish people] never forgot to celebrate [those] days" (Keneally 1975:117).

The life of Moses is not unlike that of Gandhi of India, who "in 1947, after twenty-six years of nonviolent struggle under [his] leadership . . . won freedom [for India] from Britain." It is said that "not a single Briton . . . was killed by Indians as part of this struggle" (Gregg 1969:28).

Gandhi grew up and received early schooling in India but was educated for the practice of law in London and was admitted to the British bar in 1889. A decade and one-half later, he renounced his Western ways and lived in accordance with Hindu ideals of asceticism. Although a London-trained lawyer he eschewed material possessions and dressed in loincloth and shawl. He achieved his goal, a free, united India, through nonviolent means of international negotiations and civil disobedience.

Because of his socialization and multinational education, he knew how to compel Indian princely states to grant democratic reforms and exact concessions from Great Britain. Because of his socialization and education in England and India, Gandhi qualified as a marginal person—one who lives in, between, and beyond his people (Willie 1975:46-49). He knew the prides, fears, and prejudices of both nations and how to deal with them in an effective way.

A professional, Gandhi was of the upper caste, but he lived and communed with members of the lower caste and fought in behalf of their freedom. It was his socialization, education, renouncement of vain glory, and commitment to social justice that made Gandhi a liberation leader. Education was important to Gandhi's life, but commitment also was required of the "great soul" who, in humility, became India's greatest liberation leader.

The life of Moses and the life of Gandhi were not unlike that of Martin Luther King, Jr., of the United States, who, through nonviolent demonstrations, became the great liberation leader for black and poor people in this nation. Martin Luther King, Jr., was born in comfortable conventional circumstances in Atlanta, Georgia. His family was middle class. His parents were college educated. His mother was a musician and his father the senior minister of a large black Baptist church, Ebenezer. King's higher education was in a small black liberal arts college in the South and in a predominantly white seminary and a large predominantly white university in the North. He could have become a professor, but he renounced the prestige of such a position in preference for his calling as a pastor and social activist. He became the leader of a black church congregation in Alabama.

King, too, was a marginal man. From his upbringing and early education, he knew intimately the life-styles of the black minority, and through his seminary training and graduate education, he came into contact with life-styles of the white majority. He knew the culture and characteristics of both groups and how they complement each other. He knew how to change the minds of the people in the United States—how to generate courage among the oppressed and compassion among the oppressors—because he had lived in black and in white communities and had claimed both as his own. Indeed, King said, "This is a multi-racial nation where all groups are dependent on each other whether they want to recognize it or not" (1968:61).

Through King's efforts, supplemented by those of others, the 1964 Civil Rights Act and the 1965 Voting Rights Act were passed. The Civil Rights Act prohibited racial discrimination in public places, segregation in public schools, and discrimination in hiring, as well as promoted registration of voters. The Voting Rights Act banned literacy and other tests for voter registration that disfranchised racial minorities, required federal approval of procedural changes in local election laws to protect the rights of minorities, and authorized federal registrars to enroll voters where a pattern of racial discrimination in registration had been demonstrated (Larson and McDonald 1980). These laws changed the customs and traditions of U.S. life and breathed new meaning into the constitutional clause about "equal protection of the laws" for all.

Martin Luther King, Jr., was a magnificent liberation leader because of his socialization in black and white communities, his education in black and white schools, his decision to renounce the opportunity of employment in a prestigious occupation to pursue a career of social action committed to achieving racial justice.

Despite their separation in time, place, and race, Moses, Gandhi, and King had similar experiences. Martin Buber has provided a theory of liberation leadership that embraces the way of life of these three people. He states that freedom movements are "a kind of liberation which cannot be brought about by anyone who grew up as a slave, nor yet by anyone who is not connected with the slaves; but only by one of the latter who has been brought up in the midst of the aliens and has received an education equipping him with all their wisdom and power, and thereafter 'goes forth to his [people] and observes their burdens' " (Buber 1958:35).

Neither Moses, Gandhi, nor King was the wretched of the earth. However, they all had strong connections with the people of oppression and identified with their condition. Moses was educated in the household of Pharaoh, Gandhi in the capital city of the British colonial empire, and King in a university attended largely by affluent white students. In their association with those from whom they later would demand liberation, Moses, Gandhi, and King became equipped with the wisdom and power of their adversaries. Then they turned toward their people, observed their burdens, and decided to act. Moses, Gandhi, and King exhibited great similarities in their education and in their social action.

From this analysis, I derive a new model of a liberation leader. This model is characterized by the education identified by Du Bois but education in a double culture so that one becomes a marginal person who knows and understands the way of life of the minority and the majority or the dominant and subdominant power groups. The liberation leader also is sensitive to injustice, analyzes why it exists, and resolves to do something about it. Such sensitivity and resolve are likely to occur only in those with a double consciousness—people who have renounced vain glory on the one hand and are committed to social justice on the other, people who see themselves both as they are and as others perceive them. As Buber said, the liberation leader turns toward an oppressed people, sees them as they see themselves, understands the hardships visited upon them by others, and accepts as his or her responsibility the task of overcoming their oppression. Even a person with such knowledge and wisdom is not capable of being a liberation leader unless one is able to seek a double victory that eventually can lead to reconciliation between the former oppressed and the former oppressor.

In summary, the liberation leader is a marginal person who is socialized and educated in a double culture, who has been sensitized through the development of a double consciousness, and who seeks to overcome oppression through achievement of a double victory. Education is important and essential in leadership development, but education is not enough in the development of liberation leadership. Sensitivity to injustice is needed. A proper analysis of the problem of oppression and a resolve to act are required. Analysis and action combined are essential in this theory of liberation leadership.

REFERENCES

Buber, Martin. 1946. *Moses*. New York: Harper, 1958.

Du Bois. W. E. B. 1903a. *The Souls of Black Folk*. New York: Fawcett, 1961.

_____. 1903b. "The Talented Tenth." In Leslie H. Fishel and Benjamin Quarles, eds., *The Black American*, pp. 226-29. Glenview, Ill.: Scott, Foresman, 1970.

Gregg, Richard B. 1969. *The Power of Nonviolence*. New York: Schocken Books.

Keneally, Thomas. 1975. *Moses the Lawgiver*. New York: Harper.

King, Martin Luther, Jr. 1968. *Where Do We Go from Here?* New York: Harper.

Larson, Richard E., and Laughlin McDonald. 1980. *The Rights of Minorities*. New York: Avon Books.

Willie, Charles Vert. 1975. *Oreo: A Perspective on Marginal Men and Women*. Wakefield, Mass.: Parameter Press.

Willie, Charles Vert, and Ronald R. Edmonds, eds. 1978. *Black Colleges in America*. New York: Teachers College Press.

9
The Morehouse College Saga

Morehouse College is not exceedingly large, exceedingly wealthy or exceedingly old as the years of colleges and universities are numbered. How, then, can a school that by any measure is meek and humble also be strong and great?

If by one's fruit a college shall be known, then Morehouse deserves to be classified among the elect because it produced one of this nation's most outstanding private citizens, Martin Luther King, Jr. Let us be clear about what is involved in greatness. Martin Luther King, Jr., is world renowned not because of public office or political clout. He achieved preeminence in our time because he, like the prophets of old, elected to serve and offered to suffer and sacrifice for the sake of others. The day of his birth is celebrated annually not because of his conquests and victory but because of his failures and his death. What manner of man was this twentieth-century suffering servant? What kind of college contributed to his growth and development? To answer these questions, one must examine the myth and mystery of Morehouse.

Morehouse always has taken religion seriously. It was founded by the Reverend William Jefferson White in Augusta, Georgia, in 1867. Classes were first held in Springfield Baptist Church. Originally Morehouse, known during its early days as the Augusta Institute, was primarily for the training of preachers and teachers (Jones 1967:26-29).

Any institution that takes religion seriously accepts as a mandate the bringing about of a "new union between spirit and world" (Buber 1982:2). Any institution that takes religion seriously "sanctifies everyday life" (Buber 1982:3). Any institution that takes religion seriously advocates love and justice. True to its religious heritage, the Morehouse College that Martin Luther King, Jr., experienced was described by historian L. D. Reddick as a school where "teachers encourage their students to explore and search for solutions to campus and world problems," where "nobody on the faculty seemed to be afraid to think and speak out," where "academic freedom was a reality," where student government was practiced, joint student-faculty committees worked, and "student freedom was greater than at most schools" (Reddick 1959:67-68). This is the school in which Martin Luther King, Jr., received an effective education as an undergraduate student.

It is a school where religion is a genuine source of inspiration, an antidote against the paralyzing anxiety of fear, and the basis of courage and compassion. Linking the world and spirit by way of religion, Morehouse taught its students to know what is right and to do what is right.

A school whose education is rooted in religion, which teaches its students to love and to be just, is a school that links analysis with action. It is a school that teaches its students what they should learn, how they should learn, and why they should learn. It thus imparts knowledge about new technologies and traditional wisdom. A college whose curriculum is centered in love teaches its students to reject vain pride and envy and to seek not self-enhancement but the advancement of others. Students taught in this manner are not easily provoked, do not think evil of others, but have hope, and learn to endure, knowing that the "meek shall have the earth as their possession."

Morehouse College is what it is, has been, and will be because of the dedication of those in charge. This institution and its development was the consuming passion of three great presidents: John Hope, Benjamin Mays, and Hugh Gloster. Each did for this school something unique that should go down into the annals of history as a contribution in higher education.

John Hope, southern born but northern educated, himself the issue of a white father and a black mother who married and lived in Augusta, Georgia, drew upon his multicultural heritage and made changes of long-lasting significance for Morehouse College. He helped the college not to turn away from differences but to embrace them and to synthesize opposites into a new harmonic whole. Under Hope's twenty-five year leadership as president of Morehouse from 1906 to 1931, the college embraced a double culture as he developed within the institution the courage to be a part of a unique collective educational venture.

Paul Tillich reminds us that "courage . . . is the readiness to take upon oneself negatives . . . for the sake of a fuller positivity." Moreover, "In many tribes the courage to take pain upon oneself is the test of full membership in the group." For "the self, cut off from participation in its world, is an empty shell, a mere possibility" (Tillich 1952:78, 93, 151). The same may be said of an institution cut off from participation with other associations in its community. John Hope saw Morehouse College, Spelman College, and Atlanta University as mere possibilities unless they could effect some participatory union wherein each could share the pain and bear the burden of the others, and thus achieve a greater positivity so far as education was concerned.

As a scholar of history, John Hope recognized the "cruel prejudice" that accompanies the pulling away of populations from others unto themselves. On the international scene, he characterized the absence of "courage to be a part of" as ethnocentric, racist, and offensive (Jones 1967:114). Locally, John Hope saw great duplication of curriculum and effort among the institutions in Atlanta devoted to the education of blacks. He characterized the duplication as wasteful and dreamed of coordinating the work of these schools (Jones 1967:114). He recognized the cooperating but autonomous colleges of Oxford as beneficial and wanted to establish such a model in Atlanta.

The years immediately preceding 1929 had found Atlanta University in financial difficulties, "and with the Crash [of the stock market] it might have had to close its doors had the idea of the Affiliation not become a reality" (Jones 1967:116). The irony is that it was Morehouse College that almost had to close its doors because of the affiliation. It deeded part of its property to Atlanta University, which, according to the affiliation agreement, was responsible for graduate and professional education. In return, Morehouse was to receive assistance from Atlanta University's board of trustees in raising funds for undergraduate education. But the depression came, jeopardizing the college's endowment campaign. Atlanta University's trustees were unable to deliver on their fund-raising promise for undergraduate education, and the dependency relationship of Morehouse on another school threatened the well-being of Morehouse itself.

As a consequence of its courage to be part of the affiliated institutions, Morehouse bore the pain of the Depression for Atlanta University as well as for itself. Although some new money came to the new university, the old sources of support for the college dried up. Through this sacrifice and suffering, Morehouse learned to endure.

Earlier the synthesis of opposites that characterized his pragmatic method of operation caused John Hope to befriend both W. E. B. Du Bois and Booker T. Washington. Hope was a participant in the Niagara movement led by Du Bois that resulted in the establishment of the National Association for the Advancement of Colored People. Through friendship with Du Bois, John Hope embraced the call for a classical education for black people, an education for the whole person that he and Du Bois called a "real education" (Jones 1967:83). He befriended Booker T. Washington in the matter of fund raising, for Washington was the

only black educator "capable of tapping the source of Northern philanthropy" (Jones 1967:88).

An indication of Hope's capacity to synthesize the interests of the races
in a common educational enterprise was the name change of the school
during his administration. The Atlanta Baptist Institute, the name of the
school after it moved from Augusta, was changed to Morehouse College
in honor of Henry Lyman Morehouse, a white benefactor and long-term
secretary of the American Home Mission Society.

In summary, John Hope synthesized individuals of different races,
ideologies of different educational leaders, and institutions of varying
specialties and qualities into a new and interdependent system. The Atlanta University Center consisting of Morehouse, Spelman, and Atlanta
University was stronger than the component parts. And all this was done
for the purpose of advancing the education of black people.

John Hope made several spectacular appointments to the Morehouse
College teaching faculty during his tenure. In 1921, Hope appointed a
young professor to teach mathematics, English, and philosophy. His
name was Benjamin Elijah Mays. Mays also coached the debating team.
It was Du Bois' assessment that John Hope was "building one of the
finest institutions in the . . . South, white or black." Du Bois described
the Morehouse over which President Hope presided as a place where
students were getting "sympathetic attention and first-class training"
(Jones 1967:109).

Yet Morehouse was incomplete. If John Hope furnished "vision and
culture," as one teacher put it, Benjamin Mays promoted character and
consciousness. One might describe the mission of Mays during the
twenty-seven years that he headed the institution (1940-1967) as promoting a double consciousness and helping Morehouse to develop the courage to be autonomous and self-sustaining in spite of the affiliation with
the Atlanta University Center. A double consciousness is a condition
wherein one is aware of oneself, of one's own interests, needs, and
concerns, at the same time that one is aware of the interests, needs, and
concerns of others. When there is a double consciousness, education is
perceived as having the twofold goal of individual enhancement and
group advancement; morality and ethics are linked.

One of the first official acts of Mays in 1940 in bringing back Morehouse from the brink of disaster was to teach students that they must be
responsible for their own debts, that they must pay their own way. They
could not depend on others for their survival. In his autobiography,
Mays said, "My first official act when I arrived at Morehouse was to
send a letter to each student who owed the college" and insist that the
student pay tuition and other charges. No transcripts were issued until
debts were settled. This program of discipline and self-support worked

exceedingly well and earned for Mays among the students the appel-
lation "Buck Bennie." Thereafter, when he made a speech that the
students liked, they exclaimed, "Buck Bennie rides again" (Mays
1971:177).

With the increase in funds, Mays increased the faculty and raised
salaries. He believed that "a college is not stronger than its faculty" and
gave himself the goal of increasing in number and academic quality the
Morehouse College faculty (Mays 1971:178). Then he set himself the task
of strengthening the board of trustees and eliminating the inappropriate
arrangement of the president of Spelman College, his coequal in one of
the affiliated schools, serving as treasurer of the Morehouse board of
trustees and in that capacity signing his paycheck. The president of
Spelman, who helped engineer the Atlanta-Spelman-Morehouse affiliation, was white and had good connections with northern philanthropy.
For Mays' brash act of self-affirmation, Morehouse, which some identified as the "stepchild in the Affiliation" (Jones 1967:137), was cut off
from white-controlled foundation support. Mays confessed that his
"greatest disappointment was in fund raising." He was never able to
command "large support." It was not until the last two years of his
presidency that foundations were beginning to judge Morehouse on the
basis of "the quality of its faculty, the performance of its students, and
by what its alumni contributed" (Mays 1971:191). Until that time,
Morehouse had been labeled a "Negro college," and all colleges for
blacks were classified as inferior. Some white scholars called these
schools "academic disaster areas" (Riesman and Jencks 1968:433), and
the public believed them.

Although Mays believed that the faculty was the most important component in the quality of a college, the *Comparative Guide to American
Colleges*, states that "an institution of higher learning can never be much
better than its student body" (Cass and Birnbaum 1979:xix). This fundamental difference in orientation between Mays and his white colleagues
in higher education made the fulfillment of his mission more difficult.
But Mays persevered and tried to strengthen his students to do the same
by strengthening the faculty. Mays taught his students the significance of
self-affirmation, the courage to act as oneself, to stand apart from the
crowd, if necessary, not for the purpose of self-actualization and getting
ahead but for the purpose of serving others.

The Mays administration contributed to the continuing saga of Morehouse College as "a distinctive Black College" (Butler 1977:138). Mays
summarized his feelings about Morehouse in his autobiography: "I
found a special intangible something at Morehouse in 1921 which sent
men out into life with a sense of mission, believing that they could
accomplish whatever they set out to do. This priceless quality was still
alive when I returned in 1940, and for twenty-seven years, I built on

what I found, instilling in Morehouse students the idea that despite crippling circumstances, the sky was their limit" (Mays 1971:172). Burton Clark has observed that all colleges have roles, but some have missions (in Butler 1977:100)..Morehouse under Mays had a charge to keep and a mission to fulfill. Mays did what he had to do in the time allotted. For his efforts, Mays became one of the most honored and celebrated educators in the United States, although the honors were late in coming.

Addie Butler called the distinctive black college an "endangered species" (Butler 1977:163). Hugh Gloster, himself a Morehouse graduate, assumed the mantle of leadership for the Morehouse manifestation of this species when he became president in 1967. For a decade and a half, he guided the college through the turbulent concluding years of the 1960s to the 1980s. He consolidated the trend toward assembling a high-quality faculty and greatly expanded the physical plant and the student body. What Du Bois said more than half a century ago was echoed during the Gloster administration. Morehouse continued to be a predominantly black college with a predominantly black faculty where students received sympathetic attention and a first-class education (Du Bois 1924).

Hugh Gloster did more than to consolidate and to expand: he introduced a new theme, that of the double victory, wherein that which benefits Morehouse benefits the entire Atlanta University Center and wherein that which benefits blacks also benefits whites. Gloster will be recognized in years to come for his courageous and daring decision to launch the Morehouse Medical College, against great odds, as one of the most beneficial innovations in higher education. For a school that takes seriously its religious heritage and the Jewish-Christian tradition that the anointed are sent to help the poor, to heal the brokenhearted, and to set at liberty those who are bruised (Luke 4:18), how could Morehouse ignore the unfulfilled health care needs of this nation, especially as these needs are found among black, brown, and poor people? A school with a mission rooted in the love and justice of religion could not know what is right and then fail to do what is right.

Oliver Wendell Holmes said in 1869, two years after the founding of Morehouse College, that "the state of medicine is an index of the civilization of [a] . . . country . . . one of the best, perhaps, by which it can be judged" (quoted by MacLeish 1978). Marlene MacLeish characterized the School of Medicine initiated at Morehouse as "a response to a century old system of medical education which has neither delivered a fair share of black physicians to care for the black population, nor produced enough white physicians to serve the health needs of blacks, on par with the health care delivered to white Americans" (MacLeish 1978:175).

Morehouse delineated the need for minority physicians and was willing to pursue the issue from the base of a historically black institution. According to MacLeish, this was the major strength of the Morehouse feasibility study for a new medical school (MacLeish 1978:181).

Morehouse negotiated an effective relationship with Emory, Howard, and Meharry medical schools and with other institutions. These medical schools agreed to take Morehouse medical students into their third- and fourth-year clerkship programs. These arrangements were essential in implementing the idea of a new medical school before it became a four-year school. What is unique about this innovation in higher education is that Hugh Gloster, the Morehouse board of trustees, and first dean and president Louis Sullivan nurtured this proposal into reality when others said it could not be done.

The new School of Medicine at Morehouse was an extension of the vision of a double culture that John Hope introduced in that the school eventually was linked as an autonomous institution with others in the Atlanta University Center and drew to itself a diversified faculty and student body unlike those of any predominantly white institution in the United States. The new School of Medicine was a fulfillment of the concept of a double consciousness advocated by Benjamin Mays. It had as its mission fulfillment of the health care needs of blacks, as well as fulfillment of the health care needs of all the people in the Southeast.

The new School of Medicine was a manifestation of the idea of a double victory that has been a unique characteristic of the administration of Hugh Gloster. While existing as a means of fulfilling the mission of Morehouse, the new School of Medicine added an important and significant resource to the Atlanta University Center. The new school increased the number of minority health care professionals and also educated members of the majority.

In his singleminded devotion to bring into being a third predominantly black medical school, Hugh Gloster was in temporary violation of the Atlanta-Spelman-Morehouse affiliation agreement. According to that agreement, graduate and professional education was a prerogative of Atlanta University, and undergraduate education was reserved for Spelman and Morehouse. Nevertheless, such action was in conformity with the religious heritage of the school to help and to heal. Morehouse College had the courage to be itself and to go against the grain if necessary. It also had the courage to cooperate with the other institutions. Thus it gave birth to the School of Medicine at Morehouse and then set it free as the Morehouse School of Medicine with its own president and board of trustees. In this action, Morehouse did what few nations have been wise enough to do: "It exhibited the statesmanship to know the right time and the manner of yielding what is impossible to keep" (Willie 1978:77).

I predict that Hugh Gloster will be honored for what he has done in carrying out the mission of the college and also for his driving spirit that contributed to the founding of the Morehouse School of Medicine.Those whose lives might have been lost without adequate medical care are silently grateful for the dedication of Hugh Gloster to their welfare and to the health of the nation.

Morehouse, the little school, the predominantly black school, the relatively poor school that had a vision of the double culture, that advocated a double consciousness, and that sought a double victory finally is the first of all because it has tried to be the servant of all.

Several decades ago, I sat in Sale Hall Chapel of Morehouse College as a third-year student and president of the junior class. On the appointed day when the president of the senior class challenged the remaining students to carry on the great traditions of the past, I arose from my seat and responded: "Now abideth Yale, Harvard, and Morehouse—these three; but the greatest of these must be Morehouse." In 1947, I was a young child; I spoke as a child; I was only nineteen years old. Returning to the campus an older and perhaps wiser person with decades of hindsight, I am persuaded to abide by the wisdom of my youth. The myth and mystery of Morehouse is that it continues to be the greatest of all because it continues to aspire to be the servant of all. If ever it should lose this aspiration, it will become just another college.

REFERENCES

Buber, Martin. 1982. *On the Bible*. New York: Schocken Books.

Butler, Addie Louise Joyner. 1977. *The Distinctive Black College: Talladega, Tuskegee, and Morehouse*. Metuchen, N.J.: Scarecrow Press.

Cass, James, and Max Birnbaum. 1979. *Comparative Guide to American Colleges*. 9th ed. New York: Harper.

Cook, Samuel Du Bois. 1978. "The Socio-Ethical Role and Responsibility of the Black-College Graduate." In Charles Vert Willie and Ronald R. Edmonds, eds., *Black Colleges in America*, pp. 51-67. New York: Teachers College Press.

Du Bois, W. E. B. 1924. "The Dilemma of the Negro." *American Mercury* (October).

Fletcher, Joseph. 1966. *Situation Ethics*. Philadelphia: Westminster Press.

Holmes, Oliver Wendell. 1969. Lowell Institute Lecture.

Jones, Edward A. 1967. *A Candle in the Dark, A History of Morehouse College*. Valley Forge, Pa.: Judson Press.

Luke 4:18.

MacLeish, Marlene Y. Smith. 1978. "Medical Education in Black Colleges and Universities in the United States of America." Ed. D. dissertation, Harvard University.

Mays, Benjamin E. 1971. *Born to Rebel*. New York: Charles Scribner's Sons.

Merrill, Charles. 1978. "The Board of Trustees and the Black College." In Charles Vert Willie and Ronald R. Edmonds, eds., *Black Colleges in America*, pp. 167-76. New York: Teachers College Press.

Rawls, John. 1971. *A Theory of Justice*. Cambridge, Mass.: Harvard University Press.

Reddick, L. D. 1959. *Crusader without Violence: A Biography of Martin Luther King, Jr*. New York: Harper.

Riesman, David, and Christopher Jencks. 1968. *The Academic Revolution*. Garden City, N.Y.: Doubleday.

Tillich, Paul. 1952. *The Courage to Be*. New Haven: Yale University Press.

Willie, Charles Vert. 1978. *The Sociology of Urban Education*. Lexington, Mass.: Lexington Books.

10
On Diversity
and High Quality

In diversity there is strength. The Harvard College student body is a living example that this is so. Population genetics has discovered that a polymorphic population is capable of dealing with its environment better than one that is homogeneous. Thus higher education institutions should not attempt through admissions practices and procedures to clone a contemporary student body in the image of one that existed in yesteryear, even if it could. A cloned student population would be vulnerable to changing circumstances and might not manifest the variety of skills necessary for successful adaptation. The characteristics of students in years gone by that were extraordinary could be deficient for the requirements of today.

The contemporary Harvard College student body is not fashioned in the image of its alumni and alumnae, as some might believe. Less than one out of every two offspring of graduates of the college who apply is admitted. Sons and daughters of graduates are only 20 percent of the entering class. Years ago, the matriculation of intergenerational relatives in the college probably was more evident. Henry Adams said that "for generation after generation, Adamses and Brookes and Boylstons and Gorhams had gone to Harvard College" (Adams 1964:58). "All went," he said, "because their friends went there, and the College was their ideal of self-respect" (Adams 1964:59). The deficiency of a more or less homogeneous student body was acknowledged by Henry Adams: "It is more than a chance that boys brought up together under like conditions have nothing to give each other " (Adams 1964:60). Such students are pleasant to live with, according to Adams. But one wonders what else they contribute to the learning environment.

Frederick Hart, a University of New Mexico Law School dean, has advanced two broad principles he believes should be the basis of admissions decisions. The admissions process should accept individuals who will enrich the educational experience of the school by their talents and viewpoints and those who will best serve society upon graduation (Hart 1974:400). Hart's principles are applicable to the admissions process at all levels of higher education, including baccalaureate and postgraduate study. When these principles are incorporated in admissions decisions, a diversified student body is one outcome.

A comparison of the characteristics of the Harvard College entering class today with that of one or two decades ago reveals the achievement of a substantial diversity. When Henry Adams attended in the nineteenth century, the college could be characterized, in the words of Theodore White, as a "gentlemen's club of courtly learned men" (White 1978:41). Such a characterization would be inappropriate of the contemporary class. The Middle Atlantic region of the United States is represented by about one-third of the entering class. The New England states now rank second behind the Middle Atlantic as the source of about one-fourth of the entering class. The West and Central states encompass the home communities for slightly more than one-fourth of the Harvard first-year students. No longer a men's college, Harvard's entering class is 40 percent female. If *courtly* is considered a code word for dominant group and high socioeconomic status, these too have changed at Harvard: 6 out of every 10 in the entering class graduate from public schools; 4 out of every 10 receive scholarship assistance; 2 out of every 10 are minorities representing Asian Americans, blacks, Hispanics, and native Americans.

Harvard has become one of the most competitive schools in the United States, in part because of its diversity. If the composition of the Harvard student body had remained as it was when Henry Adams matriculated (or even as it was two to three decades ago), the school would not continue to be one of the most outstanding in the nation. Henry Adams said the students of his era were pleasant to live with because "each individual appeared satisfied to stand alone" (Adams 1964:61). Such students seldom praised one another and were without passion or pain. All of this has changed, even within a single decade, as the minority proportion of entering students has risen during the administration of President Derek Bok from 12 percent to more than 20 percent, and foreign nationals constitute about 6 percent. In his Open Letter on Issues of Race, distributed in early 1980s, Bok affirms Harvard's commitment to diversity. He states that the history and culture of minority groups and the racial problems in our society are subjects that have much to contribute to all who learn. The experiences of all sorts and conditions of people, and knowledge of their pleasures and pain, are of inestimable value when shared in a common learning environment. Contemporary Harvard is a learning environment that achieves this goal.

The remarkable fact is that in achieving greater diversity, Harvard has strengthened and not weakened itself academically. The Harvard-Radcliffe Admissions Office is on the lookout for people of "worth and genius" (to use the words of Thomas Jefferson) from every condition of life. They wish to expose such students to a Harvard education that should prepare them for positions of public trust. Sociologist Daniel Bell said such persons should be found no matter where they are and their talents cultivated for use in society (Bell 1977:607-608).

These ideas fit in well with the prescription of traditional wisdom that the first of all should be the servant of all and that the educated should be persons for others. Education for the sake of community advancement differs from an emerging view that education primarily is for the purpose of personal enhancement. If personal enhancement becomes the preeminent goal of education, the current movement toward diversity will suffer. People with this goal may attempt to make a good education such as a Harvard education available to a more limited range of people, believing that this practice would enhance the reputation of the college and in the long run enable those who go to it to retain a competitive edge over others because of the school's exclusiveness. Such a practice would return to what Jefferson called an artificial aristocracy—a ruling class whose position is secured by "wealth and birth" rather than "worth and genius." In the end, such a practice would damage the current reputation of Harvard since a homogeneous population is less able and less capable of dealing with a changing world than is one that is heterogeneous. To diminish the incredible diversity that the student body now has would diminish Harvard as a learning environment for people who aspire to positions of public trust because students tend to learn from each other as well as from their professors.

That Harvard has strengthened itself qualitatively in recent years as its student body has become more diversified is revealed by the facts. Of the members of the 1983 incoming class, 85 percent had grades that were better than those received by others in their high schools; these students represent the top one-sixth of their graduating classes. Just ten years earlier, members of the entering Harvard class represented the top one-third of their high school associates. Using class rank in high school as an indicator of achievement, one may conclude that diversified Harvard College is qualitatively better today than it was in the past so far as student achievement is concerned. This fact is important because of the numerous articles written during the past ten to fifteen years asserting that institutions of higher education (including Harvard) have lowered their standards by admitting a greater variety of learners, including an increased number of racial minorities.

A recent ruling by the U.S. Court of Appeals in a case concerned with diversity in the Boston Police Department states that "the public interest requires a racially balanced police force" (*Boston Globe* 1980:16). Should the nation accept a lesser requirement for its institutions of higher education?

The Harvard Medical School is 25 percent minority. Harvard did not diversify its college and its medical school by looking only for the brightest and the best. I am certain that the minority medical school students at Harvard did not achieve the highest standardized test scores. Nationwide, blacks average 100 points less than whites on the Medical College Aptitude Test. Yet a study conducted by the Association of American Medical Schools revealed that 87 percent of the minorities who scored an average of 100 points less than whites were still in medical school three years later ready to move into their senior year and then graduate (Willie 1982:305). Moreover, the white racial population that scored 100 points higher than the blacks had a retention rate that was only 11 percentage points higher than that of blacks. All this is to say that if we wish to diversify campus communities, we will have to cease relying on standardized tests that disproportionately exclude racial minority students.

We will not deliberately seek to make college campuses more inclusive until we come to terms with the purpose of education. As an institution in society, education is for the purpose of developing people who are adequate—good enough, sufficient to the requirements of the situation. Individuals may strive to be excellent; however, this striving must remain an individual aspiration and not an institutional requirement. Educational institutions have only the right to require that those committed to their charge are adequate. Adequacy has nothing to do mediocrity. The two are not synonymous. Adequate people are sufficient.

By accepting adequacy as an institutional goal, we are better able to maintain diversity. We will wish for diversity; we will strive for diversity; we will do whatever is necessary to maintain diversity when we recognize that a polymorphic population is better capable of surviving a changing environment than one that is homogeneous.

If you will not take my word on this matter, consult the book of our traditional wisdom. Essentially the Noah myth is a myth about the linkage between diversity and survival. Noah did not stock the ark of survivors with either the strongest in the animal kingdom or the biggest in the animal kingdom. Noah stocked the ark of survivors with two of each kind.

One reason predominantly black colleges have survived is that they have always been places of diversity. One-fourth to one-third of their faculties are nonblack. Few predominantly white colleges have one-fourth to one-third of their faculties nonwhite. Few have student bodies one-fifth to one-fourth minority. More of the predominantly white colleges need to become settings of diversity to survive. But they have difficulty achieving this goal because they tend to exclude too much in their search for excellence.

I again remind you of the Noah myth, but I also invite you to reflect upon Faust. Daniel Levinson said that Faust is the story of one who wants to be excellent, who sells his soul for knowledge—the hubris of the scholar. Levinson cautions against striving to be the brightest and the best. He said that when one no longer feels that one has to be extraordinary, one is satisfied with being oneself (Levinson 1978:248-249). This is an adequate goal for higher education. It is kept alive by the minorities. If an institution does not have a plentiful supply of women and minorities to remind it of this goal, it should go about the business of finding them. It is a school's ticket to survival as well as to high quality. Noah would approve, and so would I.

REFERENCES

Adams, Henry. 1964. *The Education of Henry Adams*. New York: Time (first published 1918).

Bell, Daniel. 1977. "On Meritocracy and Equality." In *Power and Ideology*, edited by Jerome Karabel and A. H. Halsey, pp. 607-635. New York: Oxford University Press.

Boston Globe. 1980. "Police Set Five-Year Goal" (July, 10), 16.

Hart, Frederick M. 1974. "Testimony of Dean Frederick M. Hart, Chairman, Law School Admission Council, University of New Mexico," *Hearings on Civil Rights Obligations Before the Special Subcommittee on Education, House of Representatives, Part 2A*, pp. 391-454. Washington: U.S. Government Printing Office.

Levinson, Daniel J., et al. 1978. *The Seasons of a Man's Life*. New York: Ballantine.

White, Theodore H. 1978. *In Search of History*. New York: Warner.

Willie, Charles V. 1982. "The Recruitment and Retention of Minority Health Professionals," *Alabama Journal of Medical Science*, 19 No. 3 (July): 303-308.

Part IV

TEACHING AND LEARNING STRATEGIES

11

The Education of Benjamin Elijah Mays

When Benjamin Elijah Mays was a boy, his post office address was Epworth, South Carolina. Epworth was four miles from his birthplace on a farm. His parents, Hezekiah and Louvenia Mays, were born in slavery. Mays knows virtually nothing of his ancestors. He was told that his grandmother on his father's side was sold by someone in Virginia to a slave owner in South Carolina, and that a half-uncle was shot to death in the field by a white man. Other than these acts of commerce and brutality, Mays heard little of his past. Thus, he looked to the future.

From the marriage of his parents there issued eight children—three girls and five boys. Benjamin Mays was the youngest, born August 1, 1894. One of his brothers, whom he never knew, died early. Another sibling finished high school. His other brothers and sisters attended the one-room country school with a stove in the center, but they did not go beyond the fifth grade. Mays attended that country school, too. He said that his family was poor but proud.

The maximum school term for blacks in the rural South when Mays was a boy was about four months, from November through February. Work on the farm was required at other times. Cotton was picked in September and October, and preparation of the land for planting began in March. Mays was nineteen years old before he was able to remain in school for the full term. The 1900 census revealed that half of the blacks ten years old and older in South Carolina were illiterate.

The aggression in social relations that so often is associated with frustration was experienced in the Mays household when Benjamin was young, as well as in the households of other blacks who were poor and oppressed. His father and mother quarreled and sometimes fought. His father fussed at his mother when he drank too much and sometimes threatened to hurt her. His mother always talked back, and this further enraged his father. Often the children were kept awake at night by the arguing and especially their father's loud and abusive language. Mays was embarrassed by his father's drinking. Although Hezekiah Mays when sober was a kindly man, Mays said he shivered in his father's presence and ran to safety when his father was drunk. He was afraid of his father until he turned eighteen.

I write about the childhood and adolescent experiences of Mays not to defame or cast blame but to indicate that his early socialization was not problem free. Like others in his cohort (particularly blacks), Mays had plenty of trouble.

Mays' mother was religious. Each evening she called the children together for prayers before bed. She led in prayer, and her husband usually prayed with them. Occasionally the children said short prayers too. Mays' mother had a deep and sincere religious faith that manifested itself in emotional outbursts in church. In the folk community, these outbursts were called "shouting." Benjamin Mays was deeply influenced by his mother's religious faith.

The family, including his mother and father, always went to church service on Sunday when it was held. In the community church, blacks could be free and relax from the toil and oppression of the week. In church, Mays got a sense of his significance. The people in rural South Carolina were untutored but intelligent. They told young Benjamin that he was a person of intrinsic worth and value and helped him to believe in himself. The rural church people in South Carolina helped Mays at a young age to believe that he had been called to do something worthwhile in the world.

Mays remembers the second Sunday in November when the Sunday school teacher told his parents and the assembled audience in the church that Bennie was smart and would do great things someday. On children's day in June, when he was only eight years old, Mays was asked to memorize the fifth chapter of Matthew in the Bible and to recite it to the church congregation. When he finished the recitation, the congregation was wild in its enthusiastic response; women waved their handkerchiefs, and he saw all the people standing. He never forgot that experience, the unlimited support and approval that he received from his church congregation. In the idiom of his folk culture, Mays said, "The people had put their mouth on me; the minister said I would preach; the people expected me to be different, not to do the things that other boys did" (Mays 1978:20). Mays said that over the years he continued to feel that he could not let these people down, the people of his church in rural South Carolina.

Mays began school when he was six but was twenty-two years old when he finished high school. He completed high school at South Carolina State College for Negroes, which had an academy at that time. He was the valedictorian of his class and earned a prize in oratory. He then spent a year at the predominantly black Virginia Union University in Richmond, Virginia, and three years at the predominantly white Bates College in Lewiston, Maine.

Mays said his high school teachers encouraged him and helped him plan for future study. The teachers at Virginia Union were competent and had a special interest in their black students. Mays also attributes his desire for an education to his teacher in the one-room school, his church minister, and the church people. He said, "All my teachers were lavish with their praise and encouragement" (Mays 1971:50-65).

Against the advice of friends, Mays enrolled in Bates College in 1917. He said the weather was cold and few blacks were present. He lived in a predominantly white world. He called it a new physical and spiritual environment. In this new setting, he found the "hearts at Bates were warm." There were a few incidents, of course—little manifestations of prejudice—but they were rare.

During the first semester at Bates, he was embarrassed and chagrined to receive the first and only D in his academic career. He balanced that near failure with superior performance in the declamation contest; he won first prize. Committing the oration "The Supposed Speech of John Adams" to memory, Mays won the recognition of faculty and students by his victory. Campus gossip had it that Bennie could not hope to win because of his southern accent. Mays heard that the wife of his biology teacher, Professor Pomeroy, had studied speech. He asked his teacher if his wife was available for coaching. Mrs. Pomeroy agreed, coached Mays, and Mays won. He said, "I have always been deeply appreciative when people did things for me that they were in no way obligated to do. I shall never forget Mrs. Pomeroy" (Mays 1971:50-65).

The professor of Greek also helped. The subject was difficult for Mays and troubled him greatly. Some students in the class made him the object of rather unkind amusement because of his pronunciation of the Greek words. Mays asked the professor for a conference. His teacher invited him to his home, analyzed the problem, made some suggestions, and assured him that he had the ability to do the job. With this support, Mays began to improve, and by the end of the semester he made an A.

Despite the shaky beginning, by the end of his years at Bates Mays had served three years on the debating team, was selected Class Day speaker, and graduated with honors. The desegregated educational experience there enabled Mays to dismiss from his mind forever the myth of the inherent inferiority of all blacks and the myth of the inherent

superiority of all whites. These myths were believed by many in South
Carolina, where Mays was born. At Bates, Mays said, he liberated
himself by accepting himself as a free person with dignity and worth.
The self-liberation process resulted from his awareness of his own performance. He had done better in academic performance, in public speaking, and in argumentation and debate than the majority of his white
classmates.

Mays went on to study for a doctorate at the University of Chicago.
Later he was appointed dean of the School of Religion at Howard University and eventually president of Morehouse College, where he served for
twenty-seven years. In retirement, he was elected to the Atlanta School
Board and guided it through the desegregation crisis as its president.
Martin Luther King, Jr., a Morehouse College graduate, called Mays his
spiritual mentor. This he was to King and to many others.

The story of Benjamin Elijah Mays is recorded in his autobiography,
Born to Rebel (1971), and in the chapter "The Black College in Higher
Education" he prepared for the book, *Black Colleges in America*
(1978:19-28). It is a story about the education of a disadvantaged student
and demonstrates the kinds of support from teachers, friends, and others
that are effective and sustaining. Mays said he has felt his indebtedness
to people who were sympathetic with his desire to get an education,
including his mother, his older sister and his other brothers and sisters,
his pastor, and the teachers in his life. His teachers opened new vistas of
learning, inspired him, called on him to recite and praised his performance, interceded in his behalf, gave him jobs to earn money, made
loans to him, trusted him, and encouraged him to plan his future (Mays
1971:1-8).

SUPPORT KINDLY GIVEN

Probably the most important ingredient in the education of a disadvantaged student is the provision of support in a kindly way at the time the
student needs it. The support is significant in confirming the student's
sense of self, in enabling him or her to risk new experiences, and in
sustaining him or her in time of trouble. Mays received this support and
benefited greatly from it.

Support of a student in trouble is no support at all unless it is kindly
given. Otherwise the student does not trust the source of support. Trust
is the major component that mediates a learning relationship between
teacher and student. Mays trusted the evaluation of his talents that his
Sunday school teacher made, and he was motivated to seek new experiences because of the praise he received for his accomplishments.

Because the hearts of the teachers at Bates were warm, Mays could ask
for help in a new physical and spiritual environment that was unsettling.

Receiving the help he asked for, when he needed it, and also receiving the assurance from others that he could prevail, Mays transcended his difficulties and succeeded.

Students can accept coaching and correction from teachers whom they trust. Students will risk failure by exploring new experiences if they are admired for being themselves. Students will endure difficulty if they do not suffer alone but are sustained by teachers who suffer with them, who are concerned about the students' capacities as well as the students' circumstances.

As a midterm project, I asked the students in my course, "The Teaching of Urban Students" to prepare autobiographies of their educational experiences. The students characterized the teachers most influential in their development as kind—not tough, not hard, not unyielding. Kind teachers trust their students, encourage them, treat them with dignity, and affirm their self-worth. One university student said, "My favorite elementary school teacher taught us science. I loved him because he always asked, 'Why?' and because he was very kind to us. He was a gentle man who liked children." This experience is contrasted with that of a high-achieving student who learned basic skills but felt "haunted by the fear of punishment and humiliation" from the teachers if she failed to know the right answer. The student got good grades but said the humiliation showered on those who did not answer correctly shrouded her later learning experiences "in fear, tension, and anxiety." To avoid the risk of humiliation, the student said, "I learned to be completely passive—to sit quietly in my seat, speaking only when called upon, and to always know the answer." This adaptation of extreme passivity the student described as a "burden" she has carried into adulthood due to years of anxiety-filled experiences in school.

Kind teachers urged Mays to be active, not passive, and provided opportunities for him to speak out. They praised him for his achievements, large and small, and encouraged him to accomplish more but sustained and consoled him when he experienced difficulty.

STUDENT-CENTERED AND POPULATION-SPECIFIC METHODS

Knowledge of the individual's capacities and special circumstances is necessary to student-centered teaching and population-specific instructional approaches. Kind teachers attempt to understand students and tailor learning experiences to the needs and circumstances of the individuals. This can be done by accepting each student as he or she is before attempting to teach new ways. Students who believe that what they bring to school is rejected will tend to resist new information offered.

By building on capacities already developed, the teacher provides the student with an opportunity to experience success even if he or she fails initially in the acquisition of new knowledge or the development of other capacities. Success experiences are significant components in the self-concept of students. Although Benjamin Mays had difficulty in Greek and received a near-failing grade in one course during his first year at Bates, he also won first prize in the declamation contest and the respect of faculty and students for his public speaking.

Coming from a culture that emphasized oral communication, Mays' public speaking capacity was well developed before he came to Bates. His teachers provided an opportunity for him to experience succcess in what he brought to the school despite the difficulties he encountered in other areas. Experiencing acceptance of what he brought to the situation, he was able to accept coaching and correction that facilitated his mastery of the new information offered. Bates College started with Mays where he was and took him to where it wanted him to be—an honor student who performed well in spoken and written forms of communication. He achieved because he was praised for what he did well, assured that he could master new knowledge, and helped when he needed it in concrete ways specific to his circumstances. At Bates College, Benjamin Mays experienced a student-centered education specifically oriented to the needs of a person affiliated with the population group in which he was socialized.

With reference to the folk traditions of blacks in the United States, a controversy has erupted concerning the language that they should be taught in school—black English or standard English. "Blacks knows that their language be's all right" and do not have to be taught to speak that way. Teachers, however, will have difficulty getting blacks or any other cultural or language groups to learn new ways of writing and speaking if they do not accept as valid the language patterns that students bring to the school. To reject black English with ridicule is to humiliate those who speak that way. Students who are humiliated and ridiculed tend to resist accepting new knowledge from those who reject them and their way of life.

Thus the instructional issue is whether students are accepted as they are before the teacher attempts to change them. By accepting students as they are—including their black English or other language—teachers gain students' confidence, which Martin Buber (1955) declares is the only access to a person. When confidence has been won, resistance against being educated gives way. According to Buber, a student who has confidence in his or her teacher accepts the teacher as a person, one who may be trusted. In a confidence-sharing, trustworthy relationship, the teacher also accepts the student before desiring to influence the student (Buber 1955:106).

THE TIME DIMENSION IN LEARNING

Finally, the education of Benjamin Mays demonstrates that time is a dimension in learning; each person must learn what he or she must learn in the time that is available, and the temporal learning pattern for one person or group may differ from that of another.

Mays prepared himself as an educator by participating in an unorthodox learning pattern. He never considered himself too old to learn, but he wished he had time to catch up on the reading that he had missed as a child. This he could not do, "for each passing day makes its own new demands" (Mays 1971:10).

Although he was twenty-two years old when he graduated from high school, Mays graduated from college at the age of twenty-six (Mays 1978:21) and received a doctor of philosophy degree from the University of Chicago as he approached the fortieth birthday.

The slow beginning did not deter Mays from a spectacular career: election to Phi Beta Kappa, induction in the South Carolina Hall of Fame, dean of the Howard University School of Religion, president of Morehouse College, president of the Atlanta School Board, spiritual mentor of Martin Luther King, Jr., recipient of scores of honorary degrees from Harvard and other colleges and universities in the United States and in Africa, and winner of the Spingarn Medal given by the National Association for the Advancement of Colored People. Despite an uncertain start at Bates, Mays graduated near the top of his class. His progress in time is not unlike that of other black students at predominantly white colleges.

I have been critical of the use of the Scholastic Aptitude Test of the College Board because its value is limited to predicting performance in the first year of college. Scholars connected with the Educational Testing Service, which prepares the tests for the College Board, state that first-year grade averages are appropriate as the criterion measure because studies have found no systematic difference in validity coefficients when test results were compared with first-year, second-year, or fourth-year averages (Schrader 1971:118). My study of black students and white students at predominantly white colleges confirmed this finding for white students. The proportion of such students who received grades at A and B levels the freshman and senior years of college varied less than 5 percentage points. But the proportion of black students who received such grades for these two time periods varied nearly 40 percentage points.

My study used cross-sectional rather than longitudinal data; also, grade averages were self-reported. These factors temper the certainty with which conclusions may be stated. The findings suggest, however, a temporal difference among racial populations in adapting to college as a learning environment in terms of the acquisition of good grades. The adaptation of the majority population the first year of college is similar to its adaptation the fourth year but not so with the minority. From a first year that was almost a disaster, the minority students at predominantly white colleges improved dramatically to the fourth year, in which the proportion who earned good grades was 10 percentage points above the proportion of majority students who got such grades (Willie and McCord 1972:68). The experience of minority students in my study was not unlike that of Mays: "Until I entered Bates, I had always been a 'straight A' student. During my first semester at Bates, I made only one A, and was embarrassed and chagrined to receive the first and only D in my whole academic career. In the second semester, I made three Bs and three As. In my junior year, my record was ten As, five Bs and three Cs. In my senior year, I received eight As, two Bs and one C. I was one of fifteen to be graduated with honors" (Mays 1971:57).

Biblical wisdom reminds us that there is a season and a time to every purpose (Ecclesiastes 3:1). Timing in the education and achievements of Mays differed from those of his white contemporaries. Be slow to reject those who are slow starters. In the end, they may make a mighty contribution. Teachers are counseled to be patient with students so that in due season they may be fulfilled. The education of Benjamin Elijah Mays has taught us this.

REFERENCES

Buber, Martin. 1955. *Between Man and Man*. Boston: Beacon Press.

Ecclesiastes 3:1.

Mays, Benjamin E. 1971. *Born to Rebel*. New York: Charles Scribner's Sons.

Mays, Benjamin E. 1978. "The Black College in Higher Education." In Charles Vert Willie and Ronald R. Edmonds, eds., *Black Colleges in America*, pp. 19-28. New York: Teachers College Press.

Schrader, W. B. 1971. "The Predictive Validity of College Board Admission Tests." In William H. Angoff, ed., *The College Board Admissions Testing Program*, pp. 117-45. New York: College Entrance Examination Board.

Willie, Charles Vert, and Arlene Sakuma McCord. 1972. *Black Students at White Colleges*. New York: Praeger.

12
Good and Bad Teaching

The United States is flooded with a spate of reports generally concluding that schools are not doing well. I would advise accepting such reports and their conclusions with caution. Patricia Cross states that "most of the recent reports on school reform place greater dependence on authorities to specify learning tasks, to control available options, to determine standards, and to evaluate outcomes" (Cross 1984:172). These reports "pay little attention to the creation of an atmosphere that stimulates enthusiasm for learning" (Cross 1984:172). And most of the reports show little, if any, interest in the problems of "slow learners" (Cross 1984:172). Some of the reports are flawed with the error of omission because they ignore the essential role of teachers; moreover, they commit the error of constricting education to parameters that are too narrow.

Phi Delta Kappan called 1985 the "Year of the Teacher" (*Phi Delta Kappan*, January 1985:cover). I differ with this characterization. When the proportion of teachers who believe their profession is not desirable is greater than the proportion who believe it is desirable, something is wrong. While the public tends to have a higher regard for the teaching profession than teachers have of it themselves, still only half the public in a recent survey called teaching a desirable profession. The other half had either a negative opinion or no opinion (Gallup 1985:324-25). It is hardly appropriate to call the year when such low opinions were expressed about the desirability of teaching the "Year of the Teacher."

I remain convinced, however, that teaching is important, is a desirable profession, and is the key to effective education. The rallying call "back to basics" backs away from the full range of good teaching. Teachers should not permit this to happen. It is time teachers asserted themselves by assuming some responsibility for helping to define what is effective education and what is the difference between good and bad teaching. Then the public would have good information derived from a professional source with which to make informed decisions. Without the input of professional teachers in the national debate about effective education, the public may be misled into believing, as some of the reports suggest, that control and conformity rather than freedom and flexibility will result in better education.

The best way to become informed about the issue of good and bad teaching is to ask the people who have been taught which of their teachers were good and which were bad. This is a simple approach that does not require great sophistication in research design but offers reliable results. Students in my graduate course "The Teaching of Urban Students" prepared autobiographies on their odyssey in education.

A Boston elementary school teacher said, "I was an excellent reader and a good student; so I got along well with my teachers." I classify this as a negative remark because it gives weight to Cross's criticism that the reports on schools give little, if any, attention to slow learners. Yet a public school system that has achieved 90 percent enrollment of all children six to sixteen years of age has to educate both fast and slow learners. Teacher attention, however, seems to be disproportionately given to excellent readers and good students. It is a bad teaching practice to give disproportionately less attention to slow learners who need instructional assistance. It is bad teaching practice to get along well only with students who excel.

Two of my students told about the difficulties of having their unique personhood ignored, eclipsed, and merged into a collective family persona by the schools they attended. The first story is that of a middle-aged white woman who now is a specialist in nontraditional education. The second story is that of a young adult white male who is headmaster of an independent school. Both told stories of their elementary education.

The young man said, "Until grade three, I was enrolled in a public elementary school. I was not doing very well in school. In retrospect, my difficulty stemmed partly from following a brother, four years older, who had experienced great success in this early school setting. Each teacher I came upon had earlier taught my brother and the experience somewhat proved that 'comparisons are odious.' My brother was just too much to live up to. As he excelled, I seemed to regress."

The woman had sisters who preceded her in school too. Looking back with the perspective of middle age, she recalled her experience of sibling comparison by teachers as "unfair" and "demeaning." She said that her teachers were consistently biased against her because of their opinions of her two older sisters, one of whom was said to be "bright and a hellion" and the other "bright, quiet, and very obedient." The teachers constantly asked the younger sister which of her two sisters she took after. "They never stopped to realize," she said, "that I was a separate individual with her own personality."

Indeed, it is unfair and demeaning when one's own personhood is denied by others, including one's teachers. This practice of creating a family persona and then generalizing it to all family members is a bad teaching practice and ought to be abandoned. Several individuals complained about this practice as they reflected upon their educational odyssey. Stereotypes, good or bad, are inappropriate frames of reference for interacting with individuals. The freedom, autonomy, and individuality of each person must be recognized and accepted. Collective personas of families, races, social classes, or any other group or category of people are inappropriate when used to deny the uniqueness of individuals.

A black man who works in Boston as parent coordinator in a community school said, "Discipline was strict, and teachers used corporal punishment for misbehavior and work poorly done" in the elementary and middle schools he attended. Consequently he disliked school.

Even the subjects students like or dislike are affected by their teachers. A white male teacher in the St. Louis public school system who attended school in the same system during the early days of desegregation was a superior student who also liked art. He never had a chance to develop this ability because his school taught only the rudimentary aspects of art in a superficial way. This is his testimony: "The problem with the elementary education that I received was that it was too narrow in scope. I was given the basics but little else. There was no sex education, no advanced art classes or really any opportunity to be creative. I had a talent for music and the performing arts which was not developed simply because there was no outlet at my school. Academic achievement and sports were the measure of success."

Another person, a middle-aged white male who graduated from the public schools in Brockton, Massachusetts, studied art in elementary school but learned to hate it because of the attitude and actions of his teacher. His third-grade art teacher so severely criticized a drawing he had completed that he "formed an immediate dislike for art, an attitude that holds to this day."

This same person tells how the altruistic light to help others was almost snuffed out by a teacher who did not recognize the value of promoting cooperative relationships among students. In his negative reflection about school, a third-grade teacher came to mind. That teacher "had a narrow view of education and the learning process." Invariably he finished his assignments early and responded to requests from fellow students for assistance. "On several occasions, my teacher rebuked me," he said, "and either assigned detention to me or withdrew my recess privileges simply because I rendered assistance to others." This teacher, like many others, probably liked high achievers in academic subjects but did not recognize that cooperation and altruism also are mental abilities worthy of cultivating in school.

Teachers like the one described to not recognize the significance of developing multiple mental abilities. And school systems that cut back on physical education, art, and music in order to reduce the budget are not so much emphasizing basics as they are catering to what Howard Gardner calls a unitary measure of intelligence (Gardner 1984a:26). There is no single form of intelligence that is universally always useful in human society, not even the mathematical or verbal skills of the Scholastic Aptitude Test. According to Gardner, there are "multiple intelligences." Moreover, in "a society where certain activities use a combination of intelligences, each intelligence will tend to buoy the others" (Gardner 1984a:26). For example, intrapersonal and interpersonal intelligences "enhance each other. The more you understand about other people, the more potential you have for understanding yourself, and vice versa" (Gardner 1984a:26). Thus, art may enhance our understanding of science even as science may enhance our understanding of art. A back-to-basics movement that eliminates art, music, and body kinesthetics is as inappropriate as a back-to-basics movement that would eliminate language, mathematics, and science.

Gardner reminds us that "in the real world people have different abilities and disabilities." Accepting this, "we can stop labeling one another as smart or dumb" (Gardner 1984a:26). It is true that "people can be 'smart' or 'dumb' in one area"; but, said Gardner, "this tells us nothing about their intelligence in other domains." So why should language and logic rule the roost (Gardner 1984b:700). Musical intelligence is something of value, and so is fine motor movement. Civilization as we know it today would be less than it is if Leontyne Price had never sung and Doug Flutie had never thrown a football. Effective schools recognize the value of language and logic as well as that of music, art, and kinesthetic skill. None is considered more or less important; each mental ability may enhance the other.

We know, for example, that one who is permitted to cultivate and develop a propensity toward altruism may be encouraged to stretch in the development of other mental abilities. The middle-aged woman who is a specialist in nonformal education and who felt unfairly compared with her sisters in elementary school nevertheless was motivated to do good work in school because of the recognition she received not only for her academic ability but also because of the recognition she received as a tutor. Because of her achievement, the teachers kept her after school so that she could help tutor the slow learners. This woman, looking back on the experience from middle age, said she was lucky to have been chosen to be a tutor. She liked doing this very much and said that as a result of that experience, she learned early that "life circumstances, rather than genetic characteristics, had a great deal to do with molding a person's destiny." While her skills in language and logic have continued to develop even into adulthood, it is her altruistic orientation cultivated in school in her youth that has motivated her to pursue a doctorate degree so that she may become a specialist in nontraditional education.

I shall conclude this recitation of negatives by referring to a black man who teaches high school in upstate New York. He drove himself so hard to break the caste in which he had been encased that he almost drove himself into a neurosis. He thought that he had to be twice as good as all others to get ahead. He pushed himself and got ahead but almost ruined his life in the process. This is his story:

I was placed in the lowest classes until a ninth-grade teacher saw some potential in me and requested that I be placed in the academic track. From the beginning of the tenth grade on, the burden of proof of my capability was on me. I was the sole student to break out of the lower track. I became obsessed with being successful in school. Academic success took priority over my social and emotional life. I became an academic success but a social misfit. I graduated valedictorian of my class, but I refused to give the valedictorian's speech because crowds made me nervous. I didn't attend dances or proms because I always felt as if everyone was looking at me and that I was doing something wrong.

This is the story of a tortured soul who transcended his circumstances but was not transformed into a giving and accepting person because he felt he was always on trial, because he felt he was never trusted.

Mention of trust is an appropriate idea with which to shift from a discussion of negative and bad teaching practices to positive and good teaching practices. Trust connotes caring, concern, and compassion. Any teacher can manifest and exhibit these characteristics. They may be more important than control and conformity in effective learning environments. Trusting is a way of building confidence and letting students know that they are accepted and are not on trial. My favorite philosopher, Martin Buber, states in his essay "The Education of Character" that confidence is the only access that a teacher has to a student: "When the pupil's confidence has been won, [the pupil's] resistance against being educated gives way to a singular happening: [a pupil whose confidence has been won] accepts the teacher as a person" (Buber 1955:106). The imagery is marvelous—students accepting teachers as persons to be trusted, not as gods to be worshipped or feared. Buber reminds us that "confidence . . . is not won by the strenuous endeavor to win it, but by direct and ingenious participation in the life of one's pupils" (Buber 1955:107). According to Buber, "confidence implies a break-through from reserve" (Buber 1955:107).

Many teachers with whom my graduate seminar participants studied in elementary and secondary school broke through to their students. A middle-aged white male of Irish-American background said, "My third-grade teacher consistently praised me and other students for our successes and quietly worked with us to overcome our deficiencies. She was a builder of student self-concept and confidence." Another middle-aged person, the woman who is working on the doctoral degree and specializing in nonformal education, said, "My favorite teacher was the seventh- and eighth-grade teacher. She was a white-haired, sixty-year old woman who had a wonderful effect on students. She did not separate the class into slow learners and high achievers. We worked as a group on all our readings and children helped each other. This teacher could leave the room and all hell would not break out. We knew she trusted us," the teacher's former student said. "Her faith in everyone stimulated the best behavior."

Trust and faith are confidence-building relationships. From the testimony of these adults whose school days have not faded from memory, winning the confidence of students is essential for teachers who aspire to be effective educators.

A trusting relationship, however, is not one without challenge. Challenge is essential in learning, but the challenger must never become a bully. One student had fond memories of a science teacher who always asked why. He was a challenger; but she said he also was kind. It is easier to learn from persons whom we trust and more difficult to learn from those of whom we are afraid. Good teachers in effective schools have faith that their students can learn, and they challenge them to learn in kind and gentle ways.

Good teachers in effective schools also are firm and fair. A black administrator in the Boston public schools said, "I did not have any preference for subjects when I was younger. The easier the teacher, the least amount of work I performed and the more serious and strict teachers required and received the best of my work." His response was straightforward: firmness begot good work.

Martin Buber puts the matter of firmness in perspective. He identifies conflict between teacher and student as the supreme test of the teacher if the conflict is to be of educational value. While the teacher "must not blunt the piercing impact of his knowledge," Buber advises the teacher to "have in readiness . . . healing ointment." Moreover, the teacher, if he or she is the victor as teachers often are, "has to help the vanquished to endure defeat" and overcome. Good teaching that helps students learn how to lose achieves this outcome not through reason, debate, and logical analysis but through "the word of love" or compassion.

Compassion and care was all that one student needed to help her overcome a physical crisis. A white seminar member who attended school during the 1950s remembered her first-grade teacher. In fact, she was the only teacher this adult could remember. "I remember her for what she did outside of school rather than in school. She would visit me in the hospital even though I was no longer in her room." Visiting the sick is communicating with the word of love. It is a magnificent teaching technique and should be tried by all.

An elementary school teacher from the Virgin Islands told of the loving care and concern she had received from the principal of an alternative high school when she was growing up. The school had a no-nonsense, back-to-basics curriculum. This school, like the black valedictorian who felt always on trial, was trying to prove that students at the bottom of the heap in state and national scores could be motivated to achieve. Although run as a tight ship, this school had a principal and a staff described as "extraordinary." In her autobiography, this seminar participant said, "The principal not only helped me shape my educational aspirations, she drove me to a nearby college when I was exploring opportunities for further study. My parents and I thought that the college that I visited with my principal was just what I needed. So I enrolled." Were this principal's actions beyond the call of duty, or was she merely doing what comes naturally to those who offer loving kindness and support? I know not what your judgment may be. This professional educator from the Virgin Islands, said: "She was a role model" because she was committed to the students under her care. She was also a mentor and a friend."

From an analysis of the good and bad teaching experiences that adults in my graduate seminar remembered, I conclude that an essential ingredient in effective education is effective teaching. Also I conclude that effective teaching is firm and fair, challenging and compassionate. Further, effective teaching depends on confidence between student and teacher, a confidence based on trust that students have in their teachers and faith that teachers have in their students. Finally, I conclude that a learning environment in which there is confidence encourages and respects the cultivation of many different mental abilities, knowing that one ability always complements another and that none is always better than all others. Such learning environments nurture freedom and flexibility, as well as conformity and control. Good educators know that control without freedom is tyranny and freedom without control is anarchy. Thus, conformity and flexibility are essential in effective schools. Now is the time for teachers to come forth and share their experiences about good and bad teaching as the students in my graduate seminar have done. Effective education is everybody's business. None is more expert than the classroom teacher. More should be heard from such people.

REFERENCES

Buber, Martin. 1955. *Between Man and Man*. Boston: Beacon Press.

Cross, K. Patricia. 1984. "The Rising Tide of School Reform Reports." *Phi Delta Kappan* 66 (November): 167-72.

Gallup, Alec. 1985. "The Gallup Poll of Teachers' Attitudes toward the Public." *Phi Delta Kappan* 66 (January): 323-48.

Gardner, Howard. 1984a. "The Seven Frames of Mind." *Psychology Today* 18 (June): 21-26.

_____. 1984b. "Assessing Intelligence: A Comment on 'Testing Intelligence without I.Q. Tests.' " *Phi Delta Kappan* 65 (June): 700.

Phi Delta Kappan. 1985. "The Teaching Profession in the Year of the Teacher." 66 (January).

13
Mentoring Methodologies

Daniel Levinson in his book *The Seasons of a Man's Life* (1978) talks a great deal about mentor relationships. Too often the term has been used in a narrow frame of reference and refers to teacher-student relations. Levinson states that the mentoring relationship is this—but more than this. Mentors not only teach and advise; they also sponsor. Mentors believe in their protégés. They share their dreams and experience with them their pain and disappointments. And they give their blessings to those who turn to them for information, advice, and support. It is true that mentors may be sponsors concerned with the "three Rs"—reading, writing, and arithmetic. But the mentor also is one who fulfills the three Ss—service to one's protégé, sacrifice for one's protégé, and suffering with one's protégé. Mentoring has to do not with a formal role but with the character of a many-sided relationship (Levinson 1978:98).

Without mentors many would fail. Even with mentors some fail. But mentors help ease the pain when there is failure. Levinson said that it is extremely difficult for women to find mentors. Moreover, minorities, particularly those in desegregated settings, have difficulty finding others who are willing to sponsor them as mentors. Too few professionals are available who are willing to sacrifice personal gain and recognition for the benefit of others.

Mentors provide a link of trust between individuals and institutions and nurture both until they embrace each other. Psychiatrist Edward Stainbrook has rendered a simple and yet profound idea—that in the end, people can be helped only with people. This is where the mentoring relationship begins. The mentor is a source of support, a symbol of security, a suffering servant. Because the mentor is and does all this, a trusting relationship is the outcome. Success comes to those who are sufficiently secure to risk failure. The mentor is one source of security that issues forth from a trusting relationship. The mentor is the first line of defense whose belief in another enables the other to believe in oneself.

As I reflect upon my personal experience as a student, young teacher, and administrator in predominantly white universities, I am reminded how difficult it is for minority persons in higher education to find mentors who are willing to suffer their success by providing the necessary security so that they may risk failure. Minority students, faculty, and administrators on predominantly white college campuses feel as if they are forever on trial. Too few people believe in them, in turn enabling them to believe in themselves.

In 1949, I left Dallas, Texas, where I was born and Atlanta, Georgia, where I studied for the bachelor of arts and master of arts degrees, and journeyed to Syracuse University to enroll in a doctoral program concentrating in sociology. Another student from Atlanta University had studied at Syracuse and had encountered some difficulties. On my folder, a faculty member of the admissions committee wrote: "He looks like a good student. But I would advise caution. We already have had one student from that school who did not do so well." The statement was not trust inspiring. It was not calculated to cause me to believe in myself because others believed in me. Clearly this professor at a predominantly white school gave the impression that who I was, and where I came from, was more important than what I had done or where I was going. The comment made me feel that I was on trial—not because of my own behavior but because of the behavior of another with whom I was affiliated as a graduate of the same predominantly black school. I was on trial because of who I was in racial terms and the predominantly black setting from which I had come and not because of what I had done or my aspirations for the future.

A trial relationship is fundamentally different from a trusting relationship. One is secure in a trusting relationship but fearful when one is on trial. Too many minorities on predominantly white university campuses are invited to come as if they were on trial. This was my introduction to Syracuse University. Twenty-five years later, when I left Syracuse to accept a professorship at Harvard, I had a similar experience: who I was was more important to some of my friends and colleagues than what I had done. A white sociologist whom I thought was my friend said to me, after learning I had been invited to teach at Harvard: "I wish I were black." The implication was clear: in the opinion of my friend, my appointment was more a function of my race than of my scholarly accomplishments. Such an assertion is not trust building even if it comes from a friend. Another colleague, a white administrator at Syracuse, acknowledged my appointment by saying, "I don't know whether I should congratulate you or envy you." Again, the message was clear that he believed he was more deserving than I of a Harvard appointment. Otherwise why should he envy me? Envy is appropriate only in circumstances in which others obtain benefits that should have been one's own.

The cheering squad for minorities at predominantly white colleges and universities is small and sometimes nonexistent. Some of the same attitudes of doubt and distrust about my ability that I experienced upon entering Syracuse University as a student I heard expressed upon leaving that institution a quarter of a century later as a teacher and administrator.

How did I persevere and overcome if mentors were hard to find? I was blessed with mentors before I arrived in Syracuse. They gave me their trust and support, which sustained me over the years through doubt and distrust. My English teacher, my sociology teacher, and even the college president at Morehouse College believed in me; consequently I was able to believe in myself despite the evaluation of others in predominantly white institutions. My mentors at Morehouse College supported and sustained me. I was sufficiently secure in their trust that I was able to risk distrust in a new learning environment.

By examining how mentoring is performed on the campus of a minority-oriented institution, one may obtain some understanding how it could be performed on a majority-oriented campus. During my freshman year at Morehouse, my English teacher, G. Lewis Chandler, invited me to his home for supper. Later, when he was critical of the first essay that I wrote, I could accept his criticism of my writing gracefully because he already had accepted me as a person. We had broken bread together. In the intimate environment of his home, a bond of trust had been secured. Had he not been concerned with what was good for me as a person, he would not have invited me to dinner. Having demonstrated his concern, I was better able to accept his criticism. He was less concerned with who I was or where I came from. He was more concerned with what I could or could not do. On my first essay, he wrote, "No, No, No. You are not writing what you think!" From that day forth, I have tried to say what I mean and mean what I say. I could learn from his instruction because I did not feel that I was on trial. As his dinner guest, I had been accepted. Thus, from the black college experience I learned that breaking bread together is a trust-inducing situation, contributing to feelings of acceptance.

My sociology teacher, Walter R. Chivers, was a marvelous man. An inspiring lecturer he was not. He was a help in time of trouble. He hired me on as his teacher assistant at Morehouse College so that I could earn money to pay my room and board at Atlanta University. This action strained his departmental budget. Most professors at Morehouse did not have assistants. And neither did my mentor until he realized that I needed a job so that I could begin my graduate studies. He convinced the president to fund an assistantship, and he convinced me to accept the position. To have a job created especially for oneself is a vote of trust and confidence. I was never on trial so far as my mentor was concerned. He always believed I could make the grade even when I failed to do my best.

My sociology mentor at Morehouse believed in me. He even sent me to Syracuse University by inviting the chairperson of that university's Department of Sociology to my undergraduate college campus, ostensibly to give a guest lecture but in reality to arrange a meeting between the professor and his favorite student. Through such a meeting, he thought his guest lecturer might be impressed and sponsor his favorite student for a graduate scholarship. His cunning and his calculations were correct. By the fall of 1949 I was on my way to Syracuse with a university scholarship. Because my Morehouse teacher believed in me, I did not worry about the opinion that others had of me, especially the Syracuse faculty member on the admissions committee.

Twenty years after I graduated from Morehouse, another mentor, President Benjamin Mays, was about to retire. In 1967 he received an honorary degree from Harvard University. That year I was on leave from Syracuse University, lecturing in the Harvard Medical School. My mentor kept tabs on his students even after they finished undergraduate study. He knew that my family and I were visiting in Cambridge and requested that we be invited to the commencement exercises as honored guests. Although only a visiting lecturer, I attended the luncheon for the president and Fellows of Harvard College and those who received the honorary degrees. It was a cherished experience of sponsorship two decades after I had left my undergraduate school. My college president also was my mentor. We kept in contact over the years. He was a continuous source of support in many ways.

These episodes from my black college experience have taught me the meaning of mentoring. Because I had these experiences, I understand the importance of mentoring relationships, especially for minorities on predominantly white college campuses. These experiences may be stated as principles:

The mentor must first accept another as one is before attempting to induce change in one's behavior. (On many white college campuses, minorities are given a clear message that they must make themselves lovable so that they can be loved.)

The mentor must trust another if the other is even to become trustworthy. (On many white college campuses, minorities are placed on trial and trust is withheld if in any way they are found wanting.)

The mentor must support another by sharing in one's suffering, which is a source of security that enables people to succeed by risking failure. (Minorities on white college campuses are told not to look for favors but to steel themselves to go it alone.)

Trust and acceptance and support are needed in the everyday experiences of minorities, as well as in those of the majority.

Recently I completed a study of outstanding minority scholars, *Five Black Scholars* (1986). One of the scholars I examined is historian John Hope Franklin, a graduate of Fisk University and former president of the United Chapters of Phi Beta Kappa. Franklin talked with me about the role of a mentor in shaping his academic career. During his second year at predominantly black Fisk University, he studied with a young white professor from Amesbury, Massachusetts. This young professor, Theodore S. Currier, was a specialist in Latin American history. Franklin described his sophomore year teacher as a person with great charm who became his mentor. Currier let Franklin know that he believed in him and advised him to attend Harvard upon graduation. Franklin called his mentor's course in U.S. history a great intellectual experience, one unlike any other he had ever had before. After taking more courses with Currier, Franklin said he knew what a historian was and that he wanted to be a historian.

Graduating from Fisk magna cum laude at the age of twenty years, Franklin applied to and was accepted for graduate study by Harvard University. Franklin's father, an Oklahoma lawyer whose law business had been crushed by the Depression, was unable to finance graduate study. When Currier heard of Franklin's problems, he urged Franklin to return to Nashville so that together they might find some solutions. All along Currier had told John Hope Franklin, "Money will not keep you from going to Harvard." Unable to find a source of funding for Franklin's graduate study, Currier—a young professor only thirty-three years of age—borrowed enough money to pay for Franklin's first year at Harvard.

Franklin has had a marvelous academic career; he has been president of the American Historical Association and the Southern Historical Association. He retired from the University of Chicago faculty, where he was the chairperson of the History Department for a period.

Franklin is the executor of the estate of his mentor, who died in 1979. He and his wife are setting up a scholarship at Fisk in Currier's honor. The Franklins are contributing to it and will turn over the proceeds from the sale of Currier's estate to the fund. Reminiscing about the relationship, John Hope Franklin said, "Currier was my closest friend. We started out on a student-teacher relationship but became very close friends." John Hope Franklin will always remember Currier's decisive statement—"Money will not keep you from going to Harvard"—and it didn't because of Currier's belief in Franklin and his sacrificial actions to back up that belief.

Essentially, I have described a marvelous model of a mentoring relationship. Franklin's mentor at Fisk (a predominantly black college) was white; my mentors at Morehouse (also a predominantly black school)

were black. Thus, mentors may be of any coloring as long as they accept
their protégés, trust them, support and sustain them.

Mentors not only accept, trust and support; frequently they assume the
role of intercessors (not speaking for their protégés but monitoring institutions), insisting that rules, regulations, and procedures are applied
fairly and that the full participation of their protégés in complex systems
is not impeded in any way. This especially is a role that mentors for
minorities or women must perform in predominantly white or predominantly male settings.

I share a few examples of the intercessory function from my experiences
at Syracuse University, where over a period of twenty-five years I was a
student, a faculty member, and an administrator. When I was a senior
member of the faculty as Sociology Department chairperson, and later as
vice-president, the intercessory function of mentoring for minorities
came to me.

In 1970, eight black athletes were suspended from the football team
for boycotting spring practice. The reason they refused to participate in
spring practice was the refusal of the Athletic Department to hire one
minority assistant coach to the nine- or ten-person football coaching
staff. The university had just installed a new president who had heard
about the football dominance of Syracuse in the East, powered by such
outstanding black players as Jimmy Brown, Ernie David, and Floyd
Little. When he was told about the boycott and was informed of the
black athletes' demand, he authorized the search for and employment of
a minority person to serve on the coaching staff. Although the search was
successful and the coaches as well as the players liked the new staff
person, the eight black players who forced the issue and the appropriate
action to resolve it were suspended as if the head coach needed a face-
saving device. Their suspension was unfair because other university officials had acknowledged the legitimacy of the request of the black
athletes for an integrated coaching staff and had authorized funds for the
fulfillment of the request. The specific charge against the suspended
athletes was that they had not apologized for breaching the team discipline that requires spring practice and had not assured the coaches that
they would conform to coaching orders in the future.

In U.S. society, usually there is a trail of paper associated with the
resolution of serious issues. The charges, the countercharges, and the
consensus that may be reached are all recorded on paper as precedents
that govern future actions. The coaches had recorded their charges of
insubordination and violation of team discipline. But the athletes'
countercharges and their proposals for resolving their suspended status
had never been reduced to writing and shared with the coaching staff
and the university's central administration. This is the point at which I
and other minority administrators entered the picture as mentors to the

minority athletes and as intercessors in the complex system of university administration. I inquired of the suspended black athletes if they wished to return to the team and play football during the fall semester that was just beginning. They assured me they did. I then arranged to meet them at the Black Student Center and helped them put into formal language what had been only vague charges of racism within the intercollegiate athletic program. I helped them to identify their proposals for the resolution of the issue of suspension and the conditions under which they would be willing to return to the team. I served as an adviser to the athletes and as the scribe; as consensus emerged on a proposition, I wrote down and read back to the suspended players that to which they had agreed. I then helped them to think through the strategy of presentation.

Essentially the suspended black athletes took two actions and requested the university to take two actions. They detailed their charges of racism, and they promised to submit to the full authority of the coaching staff if suspensions were lifted. (They refused to apologize for boycotting spring practice because the basis for their boycott was legitimate, as demonstrated by subsequent action of the university in hiring a minority person to the coaching staff; the head coach, however, wanted an apology.) Then the black athletes asked the central administration to lift the suspensions and reinstate them as full-fledged members of the football team and to launch a full-scale study and investigation into the charges of racism in the athletic program. The study was for the purpose of providing a cooling-off period for the minority players and the majority members of the coaching staff without any party to the controversy losing face. At least, this is the way I explained the process to the black students. With the season underway and all players reinstated, the possibility existed that the twin issues of racism in the athletic program and insubordination on the part of players might evaporate and become moot. I suggested that the document containing these charges and proposals for their resolution be delivered not to the athletic director but to the provost of the university because the unjust suspensions and the charges of racism, in my judgment, had become issues that required action by central administration.

As senior professor and department chairperson, I contacted the provost after the document had been submitted by the students, told him of my advisory role with the black athletes, and suggested an administrative response: that a promise be elicited from the black student athletes to abide by the discipline of the team and to follow coaching orders in the future, that this promise be accepted as if it were an apology but that no formal apology be required, and finally that the eight black athletes be fully reinstated as members of the varsity football team. I also suggested that a university-sponsored investigation should be launched to provide a cooling-off period with none able to claim victory or defeat until the investigation was completed in a report, possibly in the spring. I explained the rationale for these actions to the provost and informed him that I was available to interpret the wisdom of the course of action proposed to others if he thought such a discussion would be helpful.

Before helping the eight minority athletes articulate their grievance and formulate proposals for their resolution, I had taken an earlier action. As a department chairperson, I served on the executive committee of the College of Arts and Sciences, the most powerful college in the university. At the first meeting of the executive committee after suspension of the black athletes had been announced publicly, I refused to let the meeting proceed with the usual business. I made a nuisance of myself and frankly looked quite foolish in raising the matter in that forum with feeling rather than before the Athletic Board. I persisted, insisting that the College of Arts and Sciences, in which most of the athletes matriculated, ought to be concerned about the suspension as an educational matter of injustice. My strategy was to get a redefinition of the issue as one that involved the total university rather than to let it continue only as an Athletic Board policy pertaining to the authority of the coaching staff to discipline football players. Most members of the executive committee said they had heard of the suspensions and considered them to be a minor matter that involved the Athletic Department only. But after witnessing how incensed and even enraged I was, one or two members of the committee and the dean said they began to rethink their positions.

After the black athletes had delivered their document to central administration and I had consulted with the provost, a great surprise lay in wait for me and the black athletes the next day. The central administration followed my advice and launched the study that could provide a cooling-off period, but it refused to reinstate the black athletes. This action not only was a disappointment to the minority student athletes, it was totally unacceptable to me. It was clear and presented evidence of the victims' being punished for pointing out the racism that was pervasive in the university's athletic program. What enraged me is that the university took corrective action—diversified its coaching staff—and then punished the students who informed the university of the need to rid itself from the evil of racism.

I had to decide whether I wanted to work for a university that acknowledged it was racist and took corrective steps but then punished the individuals—the victims—who brought the bad news. I decided to go public and to suspend all private intercessory negotiations. One consequence of going public was that I probably would eventually resign, for the delicate bond of loyalty and trust between me and the institution would have been shattered. Because of the consequence for me and the institution, I gave central administration a final chance to change its policy regarding suspension of the black athletes. I prepared a news release that rang with rhetoric and had a cadence designed to get attention. The release said that when Syracuse University refused to reinstate the suspended eight black athletes, it decided to worship at the high altar of racism. I called the office of the provost and told him that the action of central administration that accepted only part of my advice by launching the investigation into the charges of racism but ignored the proposal for reinstating the players was unacceptable to me. I explained that if the investigation vindicated the charges of the black athletes, these athletes would have missed a whole season; that such inactivity for graduating seniors could jeopardize their opportunities to play football professionally; and that under these conditions, innocent vindicated players would have been unjustly punished. This course of action, I explained, was unworthy of a great academic institution and should not be tolerated. Then I sent a copy of my news release to the provost for his information and informed him that I hoped I would never have to distribute it to the public but that he should know what was coming down the pike. I told him that I was calling a news conference the next day if ongoing meetings of central administration did not reverse the policy of suspension and offer reinstatement. Near midnight, I received a call from the university's public information officer stating that I could tear up my news release; the university had decided to reinstate the eight black athletes.

So ended the drama of an intercessory action that helped black student athletes to survive on a predominantly white college campus. The action also contributed to my own survival. Two years later, I was promoted to the rank of vice-president by the university president who was provost at the time of these negotiations. From this example emerges the idea that the mentoring function for the survival of minorities in majority-oriented institutions is not always a one-on-one relationship but often is an intercessory relationship in behalf of a population mass.

The exemplar mentor who understood well the role of the intercessor was Benjamin Elijah Mays, president of Morehouse College during the period when Martin Luther King, Jr., was enrolled as a student. During the Montgomery bus boycott, when the city officials discovered that violence would not stop the protests or end the boycott led by King in the 1950s, they resorted to mass arrests. Dr. King, who was in Nashville, knew that when he returned to Montgomery he too probably would be arrested. On his way to Alabama, Dr. King stopped overnight in Atlanta to visit with his family. Understandably, his father was concerned about his son's safety and called a group of friends together to consult with him and his son regarding the wisdom of young Martin's immediate return to Montgomery. In his autobiography, Benjamin Mays reports that "Reverend King, Sr., stated his reason for calling [the group] together and expressed his conviction that his son not return to Montgomery right away" (Mays 1969:267).

Martin Luther King, Jr., said that he listened to the men attentively because they were his elders and their word commanded respect. After hearing them out, he told his advisers that it would be the height of cowardice to stay away from Montgomery when his friends and associates were being arrested; the struggle had begun, and he could not turn back. After his response, young Martin said, silence fell upon the room, and his father began to cry. At that point Martin Luther King, Jr., said that Mays began to defend and defend his position strongly (King 1958).

In later reflections upon that meeting, Mays said, "I had to defend Martin Luther [King, Jr.]'s position. Here was a man of deep integrity and firm conviction. How could he have decided otherwise than to return to Montgomery?" Mays also said, that he was glad that he had the wisdom to give King the moral support that King needed at that time. Mays concluded his reflection on that episode with a statement of admiration for his student: "I had admired him ever since he entered Morehouse [College] as a freshman; now my respect for him mounted on wings." The mentor realized that his protégé had to be free to become what he was to become. Mays' intercessory activity was effective. Martin Luther King, Jr., returned to Montgomery. As predicted, he also was arrested.

When King was killed, Mays gave the eulogy at his funeral. He described his protégé as "close" and "precious" to him. Although "fate has decreed that I eulogize him," Benjamin Mays said, "I wish it had been otherwise—that he was eulogizing me"; for "I am three score years and ten and Martin Luther [King, Jr.,] is dead at thirty-nine." In that statement Mays took unto himself King's suffering and sacrifice as if they were his own (Mays 1969:9). The mentor must be willing to suffer and sacrifice the redemption of his or her protégé.

To get close to another as is required in any mentoring relationship is to make oneself vulnerable and to sacrifice one's own safety and security to the vicissitudes of life that are visited upon another. The human community is both finite and tragic according to Huston Smith (1958:24). There is no way to redeem another from the inevitable tragedies in career development except through sacrifice and suffering with another. T. S. Currier sacrificed for John Hope Franklin so that Franklin might enroll in Harvard and overcome. Benjamin Mays suffered the death of his student whose reckless courage earlier he supported. In suffering with his student, he helped to redeem him from fear and supported the development of a life and career that has become a model for many.

Through suffering and sacrifice, the mentor helped the protégé to recognize and realize that "to race faster and faster for rewards that mean less and less" is vanity (Smith 1958:23); that the ultimate goal is service, not success; that the institutional requirement is adequacy, not excellence; and that the outcome of human service is satisfaction, not happiness.

REFERENCES

King, Martin Luther, Jr. 1958. *Stride toward Freedom*. New York: Harper.

Levinson, Daniel J., et al. 1978. *The Seasons of a Man's Life*. New York: Ballantine Books.

Mays, Benjamin E. 1969. *Disturbed about Man*. Richmond: John Knox Press.

———. 1971. *Born to Rebel*. New York: Charles Scribner's Sons.

Merton, Robert K. 1968. *Social Theory and Social Structure*. New York: Free Press.

Smith, Huston. 1958. *The Religions of Man*. New York: Harper.

Part V

FUTURE PROJECTIONS

14
Black Colleges in Higher Education's Future

The future of higher education for blacks is the future of higher education in the United States. This statement is based on the assertion that minority interests usually embrace the interests of the majority. U.S. Supreme Court Justice Thurgood Marshall said, "The oppressed had sufficient faith in the Constitution to confront the anomalies in society and to insist that they conform ·with the basic principles upon which this nation was established" (quoted in Willie et al. 1973:xxi). In more lyrical phrases, Richard Wright also asserted that blacks tend to embrace the interests of whites in America: "We black folk, our history and our present being, are a mirror of all the manifold experiences of America. What we want, what we represent, and what we endure is what America *is*" (Wright 1941:145-46).

From this perspective, then, black colleges are seen as the future developmental thrust of higher education in the United States rather than as a residual and redundant remnant of the past. Elsewhere I have reported that

the black college is an example of an institution that has experimented with different ways of involving students in relevant community experiences. At a time when students throughout the nation are calling for relevancy in their academic programs, and institutions are experimenting with various forms of community involvement, black colleges could be most helpful in indicating how to provide a relevant education. [However,] this national resource is overlooked because of the distorted prevailing view that black colleges are merely jerry-built imitations of the real thing—the real thing being the predominantly white, private, prestigious schools in the Northeast. (Quoted in Solomon and Taubman 1973:235)

Christopher Jencks and David Riesman have said that no black institutions of higher education should be rated above the "middle of the academic procession." Even at the midpoint, they would place only "a handful of well-known private institutions . . . and . . . a smaller number of public ones," characterizing "the great majority of Negro institutions" as standing "near the tail end of the academic procession" (Jencks and Riesman 1967:24-25).

Although Riesman in recent years has modified his view of black colleges and their worth (Jencks has remained silent on this topic), neither he nor Jencks has published a retraction of the earlier classification of black colleges as "academic disaster areas." The Jencks-Riesman classification of institutions of higher education has been generally accepted.

Benjamin Elijah Mays said that he saw "a subtle move afloat to abolish black colleges," a move turning into "a crusade of tearing the black college apart" (Mays 1971:192). Sociologist Charles U. Smith made a similar observation: "When the press reports on the feasibility and functioning of black and white institutions in the same city, the stories almost invariably state or imply a threat to the survival and development of the *black* school only." Further, he said, "presentation by the press and other media of the black colleges and universities in comparison with their white counterparts . . . are frequently deleterious to the public image and effective functioning of the black schools" (quoted in Willie and Edmonds 1978:208-9).

Samuel DuBois Cook, a classmate of Martin Luther King, Jr., believes that it is inappropriate to compare black and white colleges as if they were part of a single hierarchy of educational institutions. He suggests that black and white colleges may have both similar and different functions. For example, Cook said: "It is hardly an accident that Martin Luther King, Jr., was an alumnus of Morehouse College rather than of Harvard College and that the overwhelming majority of the leaders of the civil rights movement—nationally and locally—are graduates of black colleges." Speculating about this phenomenon, Cook said that perhaps black colleges "provided a social creativity, ethical imagination and motivation, a sense of outrage at injustice and oppression, a passion for social justice and righteousness, a will to a better social order. This is why they produced leaders with the socio-ethical vision that Dr. King had" (quoted in Willie and Edmonds 1978a:54).

Morehouse College developed Martin Luther King, Jr., into a person who commanded immense influence, although King never occupied a governmental position of authority. He was the school's most famous graduate and, according to Charles Merrill, former chairman of the Morehouse board of trustees, "the closest this country has to a saint" (quoted in Willie and Edmonds 1978a:170).

The description of Morehouse College and its mission that is similar to a mission of many other black colleges is not intended as a putdown of white colleges. The goal of this brief analysis is to illustrate how black colleges and their educational outcomes may differ from those of white colleges but complement them. It could be that black colleges are marching to the beat of a different drummer from that to which white colleges are marching. It is inappropriate, therefore, to describe black schools as being at the tail end of the academic procession, as Jencks and Riesman did. Perhaps some black colleges and universities are ahead of the academic procession with reference to some of their educational practices and are marching to a beat to which white colleges and universities may eventually march.

Consider the fact that the largest proportion of all students who enter higher education today start in a community college. These schools emphasize equal opportunity and open admissions (Karabel and Halsey 1977:233) and cater to white majority as well as racial minority students. The higher education system with an increased number of community colleges is beginning to fulfill the democratic principle that a college education should be available to anyone who is willing to study diligently and try hard. This principle has been the foundation of the admissions practice of many black colleges for years. Now it is being implemented in schools for white students too.

The president of the University of Arkansas at Pine Bluff, a predominantly black college, said his school "*has always* used its resources to get an education for every student who could be reasonably brought within the fold, includ[ing] the underachiever, the penniless" (emphasis added). In Augusta, Georgia, Paine College, with a predominantly black student body, described its mission as one of "tak[ing] students who might not be admitted to other institutions, and in four or five years . . . produc[ing] individuals who go on to graduate school and who make significant contributions to society." LeMoyne-Owen College of Memphis, Tennessee, with a student body similar to that of Paine "enroll[s] students who are not typically thought of as college material." The president of this school said that in four years, LeMoyne-Owen students are "converted" into people "who can compete for jobs or in graduate or professional schools." Other black colleges describe their students as "underprepared," "deficient," and with "low levels of achievement," "less than favorable backgrounds," "overlooked" (Willie and MacLeish in Willie and Edmonds 1978a:138-40). After reviewing the mission of mercy that black colleges have accepted and the extraordinary outcome of their educational effort manifested in the contribution of such persons as Martin Luther King, Jr., and others, one wonders how anyone ever could have called them "academic disaster areas."

The admissions philosophy of black colleges is being adopted by the nation at large and is illustrated by the increasing number of community colleges that are easily accessible to all (Harrington 1974:4). This is one example of an aspect of higher education for members of the majority that has adapted to the admissions drumbeat to which black colleges have marched for years. As stated by B. Alden Thresher, who has demonstrated his understanding of this principle, "there is no such thing as an unfit or unqualified seeker after education" (Thresher 1971:39).

By holding fast to the philosophy of relative open admissions, many black colleges have influenced higher education to the benefit of both blacks and whites. They have kept alive an alternative to the elitism that has dominated higher education in this nation and demonstrated that all sorts and conditions of people can learn if given a chance.

One could classify black colleges as demonstration institutions. A recognition of their function indicates the fallacy of any movement for their dissolution. Beyond the loss of their pioneering and developmental thrusts in admissions and in other activities, such as in uniting within a single curriculum a dual focus on classical (liberal arts) and career (vocational) education, the closing of black colleges would be, in the words of Mays, "the worst kind of discrimination and denigration known in history" (quoted in Willie and Edmonds 1978a:27).

In addition to what they do for the nation, a case can be made for the future of black colleges on the basis of what they do specifically for blacks. Herman Branson illustrates the value of black colleges and universities with data from the state of Pennsylvania, where Lincoln University and Cheyney State College are located. These are predominantly black schools that receive public funds., Branson discovered this:

The state-related schools in Pennsylvania awarded 12,231 bachelor's degrees in 1975; of this total, 797 went to blacks, and 206 of these came from Lincoln. In other words, more than one-fourth of the blacks receiving bachelor's degrees in Pennsylvania's state-related universities earned them at Lincoln. . . . The state-owned schools . . . awarded 14,204 bachelor's degrees, of which only 533 were to blacks. Of those, 350 were from Cheyney. If Cheyney and Lincoln did not exist, there would be far fewer blacks in that state with college degrees. (H. Branson in Willie and Edmonds 1978:151)

The pattern observed in Pennsylvania (black schools graduating a disproportionate number of enrolled black students compared to the proportion of enrolled blacks graduating from predominantly white schools) has been seen elsewhere. A black college president said, "Black colleges are and have been a critical national resource" (C. Willie and M. MacLeish in Willie and Edmonds 1978a:147).

In *Brown v. Board of Education*, the U.S. Supreme Court stated, "It is doubtful that any child may reasonably be expected to succeed in life if he is denied the opportunity of an education." Black colleges have played a fundamental role in enlarging the population of blacks with college degrees. The significance of this action is indicated by Jerome Karabel, who states that "Americans . . . not only believe in the possibility of upward mobility through education, but have also become convinced that, in a society which places considerable emphasis on credentials, the lack of the proper degrees may well be fatal to the realization of their aspirations. In recent years higher education has obtained a virtual monopoly on entrance to middle and upper level positions in the class structure" (J. Karabel in Karabel and Halsey 1977:233). Black colleges continue to award a disproportionate number of college-degree credentials to blacks despite the increasing number of blacks enrolled in white institutions. This is so because discrimination continues to exist in higher education. The U.S. Commission on Civil Rights reports that "although almost all groups have increased the percentages of their populations having completed a college education, these increases do not match the increase for majority males" (U.S. Commission on Civil Rights 1978:16). Thus the black colleges are needed to assist blacks toward the goal of educational parity with whites in proportion of college graduates.

The college-going habits of blacks and other racial minorities are similar to those of whites for the age category twenty to twenty-four years and even surpass whites proportionately for persons eighteen and nineteen years of age. Yet the proportion of college graduates among whites twenty-five to twenty-nine years (24 percent) is nearly twice as great as the proportion of blacks of the same age group (13 percent) (Karabel 1977:137). These data are further evidence that although the proportion of blacks enrolled in predominantly white colleges has increased during the past decade or so, the proportion that graduates continues to be unequal to that of whites.

The future of black colleges, however, will not be assured if these colleges appeal to the nation for support primarily on the basis of what they can do for blacks. Branson said, "I am afraid that the high level of concern for blacks is past" (H. Branson in Willie and Edmonds 1978a:151). Expressing a similar sentiment, I pointed out in testimony before the U.S. Commission on Civil Rights, "I've lived a long time as a black person and I know . . . that it's very seldom that people are concerned about me unless there is some other investment they have in me other than just my own well-being." The point is that "we will never get good schools until all people throughout the city have some investment in all of the schools" (Willie 1978b:xiv). The same may be said for black institutions of higher education. They will never receive the support they deserve until the nation recognizes that it is in the interest of all to keep predominantly black schools alive.

Black colleges serve the national interest and therefore deserve the nation's support. Education, according to Thomas Jefferson, is for the purpose of promoting participation in public affairs. Jefferson said that education should provide the masses with "virtue and wisdom enough to manage the concerns of society" (Jefferson 1813).

Over the years education, and particularly higher education, has drifted toward becoming an elitist system. The purpose of education has shifted from that of promoting community welfare to that of facilitating individual opportunity. With these changes, educational credentials are looked upon as admission tickets to careers (*Report on Higher Education* 1971:42). Under these conditions, the contribution of education to a sense of community is less valued.

Theodore H. White mentioned this kind of education and what it has accomplished at Harvard. He identified the presidency of James B. Conant as the period when Harvard moved toward preeminence:

Conant wanted to make Harvard something more than a New England school; he wanted its faculty to be more than a gentlemen's club of courtly learned men, wanted its student body to be national in origin. Excellence was his goal, and in the end, 20 years later, when he left in 1953, his insistence on excellence had made Harvard the most competitive school in American scholarship, a meritocracy in which *students and professors vied for honors with little mercy or kindness.* (White 1978:4; emphasis added)

What does it profit a person to attend a preeminent institution and receive an excellent education that is devoid of mercy and kindness? If in learning one is not taught how to be kind, just, merciful, and forgiving, then it would be better if the learned had remained ignorant.

The black experience in higher education has as one of its major missions the promoting of the general welfare. To do this, colleges and universities must teach their students how to turn toward rather than against one another. Where there is true education, there is real encounter, genuine exchange, and a sense of community.

"Perhaps the greatest and most distinctive contribution of black colleges to the American philosophy of higher education," according to Gregory Kannerstein, "has been to emphasize and legitimate public and community service as a major objective of [a college education]. . . . The black colleges view educational excellence and community service as inextricably intertwined" (G. Kannerstein in Willie and Edmonds 1978a:31). By keeping the goal of promoting the common good alive as an outcome of higher education, black colleges serve the entire nation.

Black colleges have a major responsibility to help higher education overcome an obsession with preeminence and to help the nation return to its basic values of freedom, equality, and democracy. These are the basics to which we should return. Kannerstein has pointed out that there is "the seeming obsession of black colleges with democracy and citizenship." A review of their official literature, he said, reveals "a frequent litany of 'education-citizenship-leadership-democracy' that affirms a belief in the democratic process and in the ability of colleges, students, and alumni to influence it" (G. Kannerstein in Willie and Edmonds 1978a:39). Black colleges are uniquely capable of performing this service for the nation because their students, faculty, and administrators have not become so accustomed to freedom and equality that they no longer value them.

Thus, black colleges must be saved so that they can help save the nation. They can help save the nation by demonstrating how to desegregate minority and majority students, faculty, and staff; how to mediate the self-interests of minority and majority groups and accommodate their different perspectives; and how to integrate the goals of minority and majority populations so that victory for the former oppressed also is victory for the former oppressors. These are unique functions of the minority, to whom the majority must turn for help.

REFERENCES

Harrington, T. 1974. *Student Personnel Work in Urban Colleges*. New York: Intext Press.

Jefferson, Thomas. 1813. "Letters to John Adams on Natural Aristocracy." In Stuart Gerry Brown, ed., *We Hold These Truths*, pp. 114-18. New York: Harper.

Jencks, Christopher, and David Riesman. 1967. "The American Negro College." *Harvard Education Review* 37 (Winter), 3-60.

Karabel, Jerome, and A. H. Halsey, eds. 1977. *Power and Ideology in Education*. New York: Oxford University Press.

Mays, Benjamin E. 1971. *Born to Rebel*. New York: Charles Scribner's Sons.

Solomon, L., and P. Taubman. 1973. *Does College Matter?* New York: Academic Press.

Thresher, B. Alden. 1971. "Uses and Abuses of Scholastic Aptitude and Achievement Tests." *Barriers to Higher Education*, pp. 24-40. Edited by College Entrance Examination Board. New York: College Entrance Examination Board.

U.S. Civil Rights Commission. 1978. *Social Indicators of Equality for Minorities and Women*. Washington, D.C.: Government Printing Office.

White, Theodore H. 1978. *In Search of History*. New York: Warner Press.

Willie, Charles Vert. 1978b. *The Sociology of Urban Education*. Lexington, Mass.: Lexington Books.

Willie, Charles Vert, and Ronald R. Edmonds, eds. 1978a. *Black Colleges in America*. New York: Teachers College Press.

Willie, Charles Vert, et al. 1973. *Racism and Mental Health*. Pittsburgh: University of Pittsburgh Press.

Wright, Richard. 1941. *12 Million Black Voices*. Salem, N.H.: Ayer.

15

The Future of Desegregated Elementary and Secondary Education

Some educators believe that the school of the future may change from being an agency within which the child is taught to being the agent responsible for seeing that the child learns. Such beliefs emphasize the effects of schooling and deemphasize the educational process. I believe that emphasis on outcome only misreads the past and present functions of education and represents a distortion of its future.

President Lyndon B. Johnson's Howard University speech in 1965 announced a White House Conference on Civil Rights to develop a blueprint for action that would help U.S. blacks to move beyond opportunity to achievement. Daniel Patrick Moynihan has been identified as a principal adviser to Johnson's speechwriter for that occasion. The theme of moving from opportunity to achievement is the rhetoric of the elitists who see education as a product rather than a process.

Equal educational achievement is not what the civil rights movement was about. This movement, which resulted in multiple federal court orders to create unitary public school systems, was for the purpose of eliminating inequality in the distribution of educational resources. Eliminating institutional inequality was the mission of the 1950s, 1960s, and 1970s. It was a movement for the achievement of corporate justice as described by Joseph Fletcher (1966:90). Corporate justice has to do with mutual obligations between majority and minority populations. Corporate justice is different from distributive or contributive justice. The latter two have to do with the obligations of many to one or of one to many.

Equal educational opportunity for a plurality of population groups means that each group will be provided an opportunity to learn how to function in a way that fulfills its self-interests for the common good and that society will make it possible for each to become what it is capable of becoming—nothing more but also nothing less. To date, few members of minority groups, racial or otherwise, have had the opportunity to become all that they are capable of being.

The attempt to define equal achievement publicly as the new goal of public education is a desperate final effort by the elitists to control public education on their own terms. Their effort is manifested most visibly in the minimal competency testing programs that establish a common standard of achievement for high school graduates. These tests are designed by the elite. I predict that they will create a momentary flurry but eventually will fade away, since elitist dual public school systems that supported exclusion are being eliminated through increased desegregation and the legal requirement of unitary status.

The elitists' techniques that excluded racial minorities in the past oppressed other subdominant populations too. Physically handicapped students and female students have benefited from school desegregation as much as—and in some instances more than—the racial minority groups. These groups, in alliance with the racial minorities, will not tolerate the establishment of another elitist approach to education, such as minimum competency testing, that does not take cognizance of the different experiences and intelligences of individuals.

Education as a process is compassionate, embraces the principle of differences, and asks no one to be more than he or she is capable of becoming but respects each person for what he or she was, is, and hopes to be. This approach to public education will recognize that learning, not achievement, is the essence of education and that important learning can occur in situations of failure as well as success. Learning is an activity that occurs by way of direct and indirect relationships. It is a process, not a product.

Court-ordered racial desegregation has shaken the foundations of education and has prepared it for change.

The late James Allen, former commissioner of education in New York State, acknowledged the significant contribution of minorities to educational reform in this century in his testimony before the U.S. Commission on Civil Rights. He said, "I think Negroes in their demonstrations, in their peaceful demonstrations, have done more than any other segment of our society to push us to the point where we have now gone. I would urge that they . . . continue to make known to the American people that there are deprivations" (*Hearing before the U.S. Commission on Civil Rights*, 1967:207). The minorities in our midst today are continuing a grand tradition of creative dissent that was manifested in such events as the Boston Tea Party two centuries ago. The dissent then and now has had the same goal and method: the establishment of a democratic nation dedicated to justice and liberty for the general welfare of all citizens.

A problem is that many policy makers do not have the wisdom of James Allen and therefore do not recognize the beneficial effects of creative dissent by contemporary minorities because these minorities are unlike the majority. Today those who dream of a democratic nation dedicated to justice and freedom for all are black and brown people, young and poor people. They are the minorities who probably represent the interests and ultimate educational values of this nation more effectively than the affluent white majority. Daniel Patrick Moynihan, who said that it is disadvantageous for a minority group to operate on a series of principles that differs from the majority group, clearly did not understand the value of minorities as creative dissenters. Despite the limited perspective, wisdom, and understanding of the function of minorities in our society by some of our most influential policy makers, minorities have continued as loyal opposition—a necessary role that pushes for appropriate change or stability.

Desegregation in urban education has been the most visible institutional change that the racial minorities have pressed on the nation. They did this by refusing to conform to an educational system that had become progressively unequal in services rendered to its citizens. If they had listened to Moynihan and ignored their calling to creative dissent, the public schools in the United States would have become increasingly segregated, and the method of universal education for the goal of enhancing informed participation by all in a republican form of government eventually would have been displaced. The racial minorities cut off this movement by their dissent, by ceasing to cooperate in their own oppression, and by taking their case against unequal education to the court for a judicial decision. They won. Because the minorities won, the nation also won; desegregated public education continues to serve as a way of including all people in public affairs in contrast to segregated public education, which tends to exclude.

By desegregating public education in cities, the minorities have started or revived a process that the majority will have to complete in the suburbs. In the *Brown v. Board of Education* decision of 1954, the U.S. Supreme Court described an equitable educational process as one in which a student of one racial group is able "to engage in discussion and exchange views with other students." Racial segregation prohibits this kind of exchange between black and white students so that the Court therefore declared it to be unlawful in public education. The same could be said for social class segregation.

Education, like water and wood, is a national resource, but unlike the material national resources, education does not have an exhaustible quantity. When some people have more material resources, others have less. Some have viewed education as a resource that conforms to a distributive pattern similar to that of other material resources. Such an analogy when applied to education is wrong. Actually education has a transcendent quality like justice in which there is none for anyone unless there is some for everyone. The same cannot be said for water and wood and other physical resources. They can be hoarded but education and justice cannot. They increase in value for anyone to the extent that they are possessed and shared by all.

Court-ordered racial desegregation in public schools already is beginning to teach this generation of students important information about constitutional law and corporate justice. Such learning could benefit students who live in communities segregated by social class. Education in a setting of social class segregation fosters attitudes of entitlement untempered by concerns about corporate justice. This kind of education is deficient.

I predict that people who study carefully the racial desegregation movement in urban education will realize its potential educational benefits for all and will undertake efforts in the future to extend this important learning to suburbs by dismantling social class segregated schools. Integrated education by social class is the reform for the future that has been stimulated by the movement for desegregated racial education today. Desegregated social class education will be achieved by eliminating laws in suburban communities that mandate lot size for home construction, by extending mass transportation systems to suburban areas so that automobiles are not required to go to and from work, by the development of cooperative programs between city and suburban school systems and even the consolidation of some into a single school district, and by federal and state housing policies and programs that will make subsidized housing available in the suburbs as well as in the cities.

Institutional systems, including educational systems, tend to change as new concepts become part of them and are implemented; as existing members of the system assume new roles and thereby assume new duties, responsibilities, and obligations toward others; and as new clients with new needs are taken into the system. Any and all of these developments tend to induce change within a system as it adapts to new circumstances. The presence of racial minority children in previously segregated white schools and the presence of low-income children in previously segregated affluent schools will change these institutions as they adapt to the needs of all their students—the black, brown, and white students and the lower-class, working-class, and middle-class students.

One change I predict that will come about in all school systems as a result of racial and social class integration is concern with truth and honesty as important indicators of value-added in formal education. Marie Peters reported in her Harvard doctoral dissertation in 1976 that black parents rank honesty and truthfulness in their children as more important than getting good grades in school.

The resignation of Richard M. Nixon as president of the United States was related to truth and honesty more than to intelligence as manifested in verbal and mathematical aptitude. The resignation was a disgrace for him and probably a national tragedy for all of us. Certainly his performance as a national leader did not reflect glory upon the educational system of this nation which had tended toward a meritocracy. President Nixon was a product of this meritocratic educational system. He was recognized as a good student and he graduated from Duke University Law School near the top of his class. He was an able speaker, competent in terms of verbal skills, intelligent, and well informed. Yet he had to resign from the highest office of this nation because he was untruthful and dishonest. This is not my personal judgment. It is that of Patrick J. Buchanan who was assistant to the president, speechwriter, and personal friend. According to Bob Woodward and Carl Bernstein (1976), Buchanan said to Nixon's daughters and their husbands: "The problem is not Watergate or the cover-up. It's that [the president] hasn't been telling the truth to the American people. The tape makes it evident he hasn't leveled with the country for probably eighteen months. And the President can't lead a country he has deliberately misled for a year and a half." John Dean, counsel to the president, said that he was stunned with the authoritative way the president responded to a reporter's "very polite question about Watergate" at a news conference on August 29, 1972. Dean was stunned by the way the president had "plowed into it with such bold lies." Later Dean said to himself, "What a performance. That's what it takes to be on the first team" (Dean 1977:125). This is one of the outcomes of a meritocratic educational system that views education as a product and that considers verbal facility more important than truth and honesty. Later John Dean changed his opinion of the president. The process of events that changed his mind were initiated by a black service worker in the Watergate office building who discovered the illegal break-in by persons associated with the Committee to Reelect the President.

The goals of education in the future will be radically changed in integrated schools to accommodate the goals of black parents who rank honesty and truthfulness as important as getting good grades. The goals of schools that will have black as well as white students because of desegregated education of necessity will have to adapt to the needs of their new clients. The education of all will prosper in the future because of the adaptations of the schools to these new students.

Desegregated education probably will spread from the cities to the suburbs and will include social class as well as racial integration. Along with these new schools of pluralistic populations will come new educational goals that emphasize truth and honesty, as well as proficiency in communication and calculation skills. These changes will occur as the minorities of this nation, whomever they may be, continue to practice the grand tradition of serving as creative dissenters and as they insist that this nation live up to its basic constitutional values of freedom and justice for all.

An important outcome of desegregated education to date has been the loosening of the hold of the social class system on the schools. At the midpoint of the twentieth century, James B. Conant, a former president of Harvard, observed that "a caste system finds its clearest manifestation in an educational system" (Conant 1961:11-12). Sociologist A. B. Hollingshead explained how it works. In a study of Elmtown's youth, he found that "upper class control tends to result in the manipulation of institutional functions in the interest of individuals and families who have wealth, prestige and power." He said that such manipulation "is justified always . . . as being in the interest of 'all the people.'" Hollingshead warned that the "acceptance of this view by the rank and file . . . will seriously hinder the development of any effective program designed to reorient the schools" (Hollingshead 1949:452).

Racial minorities have successfully rejected the meritocratic view that what is good for the brightest and the best is good for all. With the aid of the U.S. Supreme Court, they have tried to rescue the public schools from the control of a meritocracy caste system and set them free. In the future, as the distribution of educational resources becomes more equitable and formal learning becomes more accessible, education as a process will be more important than education as a product; adequacy will replace the excessive concern about excellence; community advancement will emerge as a goal of education that complements individual enhancement; and democracy rather than meritocracy will prevail.

Education in the future will be different, and so will the society it is designed to serve. Desegregation will be exalted for its role in rescuing this nation from its drift toward an elitist meritocratic social system that tends to exclude. Education in the future will be a system of genuine inclusiveness.

The liberation and reform of public education today by the school desegregation court cases initiated by minorities is reminiscent of the way that societies have been renewed and regenerated in the past. Commenting on the role of minorities in the regeneration of human societies, Richard Korn states that the majority "inheritors of greatness waste the heritage." Then Korn asks: "Who . . . is left to keep the flame alive— whence comes the regeneration?" His answer: Regeneration for the system tends to come from the oppressed. Korn further states: "This, perhaps, is the complacent bigot's most bitter purgative: in the end he can be saved only by those who survived the worst he could do to them—his victims" (Korn 1968:195-96).

Perhaps one reason that the racial minorities have been able to contribute to the regeneration of society and its schools, more so than others, is that they have continued to have hope. The *Boston Globe* published a Gallup Youth Survey conducted in 1977 based on telephone interviews with teenagers in the United States. A striking fact is that a majority of all youth, except blacks and other nonwhite minorities, believed that in the next ten years the world would be a worse place in which to live compared to the present. While nonwhites who had a similar belief was 42 percent, this proportion was 14 percentage points smaller than the 56 percent of white youth who held a pessimistic view of the future (*Boston Globe* 1978:18).

Clearly racial minorities have continued to believe in the efficacy of the U.S. Constitution. Why else would they continue to seek redress for educational inequality and other forms of injustice in the courts. The racial minorities in the United States still value freedom and justice for the purpose of promoting the general welfare. These are the basic values of this nation, more basic than is the value of meritocracy, a mainstay of majoritarian values.

REFERENCES

Boston Globe. 1978. Gallup Youth Survey, February 8.
Conant, James B. 1961. *Slums and Suburbs*. New York: New American Library.
Dean, John. 1977. *Blind Ambition*. New York: Pocket Books.
Fletcher, Joseph. 1966. *Situation Ethics*. Philadelphia: Westminster Press.
Hearing before the United States Commission on Civil Rights in Rochester, New York, September 16-17, 1966. 1967. Washington, D.C.: U.S. Government Printing Office.
Hollingshead, A. B. 1949. *Elmtown's Youth*. New York: John Wiley & Sons.
Korn, Richard. 1968. *Juvenile Delinquency*. New York: Crowell.
Woodward, Robert, and Carl Bernstein. 1976. *The Final Days*. New York: Avon.

16
Ambiguity
and Ambivalence—
Responses to Education

Manfred Stanley urges us to accept public policy discourse on education as an "invitation for intellectual activity more fundamental than technological problem solving" (Stanley 1978:216). As he sees it, "education has to do with competent personal engagement with ancestors, contemporaries, and descendants" (Stanley 1978:217). Operationally these are "the ability to speak across boundaries, the ability to help interpret the public interest, and the ability to participate in the public order" (Stanley 1978:205).

Stanley states that the difficulty in making a proper assessment of education in part is affected by a tautological understanding that "education is what happens in schools [and that] school is where you go to be educated" (Stanley 1978:192). The problem with this tautology is that it lacks a "truly societal analysis" of education and its place in social organizations (Stanley 1978:203). A societal analysis reveals that the United States is undergoing "an intensification of explicit value [on] pluralism" (Stanley 1978:195). Thus, the attempt to reduce education to the basics of helping young people become functionally literate in English and to understand mathematics so that they can get a job ignores the fact that literacy also is connected with language, and in the city several languages are spoken (Stanley 1978:194).

"An adequate philosophy of education," according to Stanley, "is ultimately rooted in a philosophy of experience" (Stanley 1978:207), the experience of all the people. This means that the stability of education should not be maintained at the expense of a wide range of ethnic, racial, economic, and gender interests in the population and that the institutional agents of education should not represent the interests of the dominant only (Stanley 1978:194).

Our discourse on the purposes and effects of education may proceed with fewer charges and countercharges of betrayal if we acknowledge that "the legitimate mission of public education [in the United States] has always been ambiguous . . . due . . . in part to the ideological barriers to value consensus posed by a liberal democratic, pluralistic market society" (Stanley 1978:189). Education is concerned with individual enhancement and group advancement—not one or the other but both. Thus the goals of education and its methods of fulfilling them must necessarily deviate in part from those of a market economy, a nuclear kinship system, a political democracy, or a religion of divine revelation. Education as a social institution is related to but also separate from these other institutions and can fulfill its ambiguous missions best when both its autonomy and its interdependence are recognized and acknowledged.

It is no secret that several institutions from time to time have attempted to dominate education and restrict its mission largely to serving their needs only. First, the family dominated education when the nation was rural and a series of interconnected but relatively isolated farming communities. Then business attempted to dominate education as workers of varying developed skills were needed to staff factories and commercial establishments in the cities. Finally, the government in recent years has attempted to dominate education and subvert its mission to that of fulfilling the exclusive goals of loyalty to the nation-state. As an interdependent institution, education must serve other institutions as other institutions must serve it. But education can be of greatest service only if it is free to be an independent institution as well as one related to others.

The wish to dominate education and its chief agency, the school, and to make it more efficient is due largely to a misunderstanding of how cities and urban social organizations function effectively. Jane Jacobs provides a helpful perspective on the city that should help us to understand how education functions best. She describes cities as inefficient and impractical, especially when compared with towns, but these deficiencies are necessary (Jacobs 1970:85, 86). Historically cities have been the setting of creativity, innovation, and development. Jacobs reminds us that "development work is a messy, time- and energy-consuming business of trial, error, and failure. Success is never a certainty" (Jacobs 1970:90). Under conditions of efficiency, the rate of well-established work tends to soar. But Jacobs has found that efficiency seldom makes a city prosper. Of its economy, for example, efficient cities do not excel in the development of new goods and services because they tend to inhibit the trial and error that characterize less efficient operations (Jacobs 1970:96-97). It is the disappearance of variety that saps the life of community (Jacobs 1970:101). Effective cities, of course, are places of variety.

Our concerns about education in recent years have been about returning to the basics, establishing standards, and increasing efficiency. These concerns are antithetical to variety. Because educational systems are existential and not ordained, we should examine carefully what we have already achieved before jettisoning it in favor of a hypothetical system that could be more efficient—but also could be less effective.

The most remarkable accomplishment of our educational system is its universality. The *Digest of Educational Statistics, 1982*, states that "free public education is available to all, . . . that in most states school attendance is compulsory between the ages of 7 and 16, . . . [and that] school dropouts before the age of 16 is becoming a rarity in this county" (National Center for Educational Statistics 1982:33). Specifically elementary and secondary education is offered by 86,000 public schools; 88 percent of the total enrollment in kindergarten through grade 8, and 90 percent of the total in grades 9 through 12 are in the regular public schools (National Center for Educational Statistics 1982:33).

Approximately 3 million teachers are available at elementary and secondary school levels to instruct over 46 million students (National Center for Education Statistics 1982:8, 11). Thus, the national ratio is approximately fifteen students per teacher, quite an achievement. These are remarkable resources, and they have contributed to a positive outcome. About three-fourths of all students who begin elementary and secondary education in the United States complete high school; about half this number enter college or some other post-secondary education; and about half of all students who enter college go to graduate school (National Center for Education Statistics 1982:14).

These remarkable achievements in education came during the period when education in the United States was experiencing its greatest transformation due to the requirements of the 1954 *Brown v. Board of Education* U.S. Supreme Court decision that outlawed dual educational systems within a common community for the differential education of students of various racial groups. In 1950, when our nation operated legally sanctioned segregated school systems, only half the students who entered elementary school eventually graduated from high school, and of that number of high school graduates, only about two-fifths (40 percent) entered college (National Center for Education Statistics 1982:15). Today, high school graduates are up from one-half to three-fourths of those who started in elementary school, and 50 percent rather than 40 percent of high school graduates go on to college. Moreover, in 1950, during the age of segregation, the nation spent only 3.4 percent of its gross national product on education. Today it has doubled this amount, spending over 6.8 percent (National Center for Education Statistics 1982:23).

Mary von Euler, formerly of the National Institute of Education, has stated that "minority groups, as plaintiffs, usually provide the impetus for legal action [that has resulted in school desegregation]. The courts provide a catalyst and leverage for change. [But] the governmental and social structures of the community constrain the process of implementation" (von Euler 1981:xv-xvi).

Minority groups have tended to serve as the stimulus to change in our education systems because the opportunities and remarkable achievements experienced by dominant groups in the society have not always been available for subdominant groups to the same extent. In 1950, for example, and during the age of segregation, the median school year completed by whites twenty-five years of age and over was 40 percent higher than the median for blacks. Today, well into the age of desegregation, the difference is less than 1 percent in median school year for the dominant and subdominant racial populations of this age category (National Center for Education Statistics 1982:16). Indeed the difference between the median school year completed by blacks over a period of three decades has represented a remarkable 75 percent gain from 1950 to the 1980s. That this extraordinary achievement was associated with the turbulence and social change of school desegregation was suggested by Willis Hawley, who reported a "dramatic 50 percent decline in the drop out rate of black students from 1967 to 1977, the period during which desegregation had its greatest impact" (Hawley 1981:148).

Desegregation was a population-specific approach to remedy the educational grievances of the plaintiff minorities. In doing this, the nation also helped the majority population in several ways through school desegregation. Beyond lowering the teacher-pupil ratio (which was thirty students per teacher in 1950) and increasing the proportion of majority-group students enrolled in and graduating from secondary school (75 percent today), other reforms were generated in urban school systems from top to bottom after *Brown*. In Boston, for example, the court order to desegregate the public schools also required the system to upgrade facilities, reform the board and administration, mainstream students with special needs, offer six bilingual programs, racially diversify the student body of the prestigious Boston Latin School, establish several magnet schools, and sanction an alliance among public schools, colleges, universities, and businesses (Dentler 1984:68, 69, 78). Moreover, the court order required a rating process for appointment of principals, a personnel evaluaton system, and increased parent participation. These benefits occurred along with the cry of outrage about the court that ordered these reforms.

These reforms in Boston and elsewhere indicate one of the functions of minorities in urban education. By stirring up things, they bring about changes that are beneficial to all. In other words, minorities "are the creative dissenters who increase our ethical stature and keep alive the vision of justice for all. Minorities are the people most likely to do this in any society because their well-being depends on how well the total society accommodates deviations from the norm" (Willie 1978:173). The minorities are our dreamers of a better society.

Blacks have made education the keystone in the structure of their freedom house. After the end of slavery, Booker T. Washington said that there was an intense desire on the part of black people for education. He said, "Few were too young, and none too old, to make the attempt to learn. . . . The great ambition of the older people was to try to learn to read the Bible before they died" (quoted in Du Bois 1935:641-42). (Parenthetically, may I say that liberation leaders among blacks today still are the educated who continue to read the Bible. When the roll of twentieth-century black leadership is called, standing among them tall are the Reverend Benjamin Hooks, the Reverend Jesse Jackson, the Reverend Andrew Young, and the Reverend Walter Fauntroy. Among deceased black heroes of recent years are the Reverend Benjamin E. Mays, the Reverend Howard Thurman, the Reverend Modicia Johnson, the Reverend Adam Clayton Powell, Jr., and the Reverend Martin Luther King, Jr. To this randomly selected list, one could add more clergy professionals. Black leaders have been and continue to be the well educated who are well versed in the traditional wisdom of the Scriptures. This is a fact worthy of remembering.)

When young people, and especially young blacks, begin to strive for prestige, power, and authority; for a handsome husband or a good-looking wife; for a big house, a sports car, and plenty of money—those who strive for these things tend to turn against religion and education, the institutions that helped to set them free. In religion there is faith. In education there is hope. All around us there are signs that blacks are increasingly ambivalent about education and religion as the source of the nation's salvation. They are attracted by other centers of power. Let me give an example.

The May 1982 issue of *Ebony* magazine listed the hundred most influential blacks in the United States. I do not blame *Ebony* for this list. Good journalism reflects the popular ethos. The sector of society represented among the most influential blacks in the United States is the basis of my concern that minorities may be turning away from the institutions of faith and hope in exchange for economic power and political authority. Among the most influential blacks,

45 percent are politicians and public servants.

25 percent direct national voluntary associations such as labor unions, professional, and social groups.

13 percent head fraternities, sororities, and lodges.

10 percent are business executives.

7 percent, the remainder, consist of entertainers, writers, foundation officers, and religious leaders.

In that list of influential blacks, not a single educator was mentioned. Clifton Wharton, Jr., is unequivocal in his statement that "in recent years, investment to develop the mind of the black community has paid off . . . for blacks." Although income differentials remain between the races, Wharton said incomes for blacks rose rapidly for persons with college educations. He declared that "education—especially higher education—continues to be a major factor in the progress of black society" (Wharton 1972:281-82). Wharton knows what he is talking about; he is both an educator and an economist. Even for blacks who want political decision-making authority and the power of money, education is the most reliable route to achieve these goals.

Of the individuals on the *Ebony* magazine list of most influential blacks, however, 70 percent are politicians, public servants, and directors of national voluntary associations. Fifty to sixty years ago, 70 percent of the blacks who had attained sufficient distinction to be listed in *Who's Who* were leaders in organized religion and in education (Lieberson and Carter 1979:352). How different black leaders are today compared to earlier years in the century!

There is a tendency among groups experiencing increased freedom to become ambivalent about the heritage that saved and sustained them and to aim at preeminence, modeling their behavior in the image of the dominant people of power. This is precisely what blacks appear to be doing as they more and more esteem the brokers of political and economic power. I do not deny that politicians, public servants, and business leaders are responsible persons worthy of esteem. My concern is that in striving for prestige, preeminence, and power, the subdominant group may be giving up on its unique heritage and most significant function in society: holding fast to the virtues of religion and education. Influential people who are conquering new and different areas and who are gaining more power and authority may be committing the error observed among the Romans centuries ago, and discussed in Chapter 2.

Some whites have recognized this fact and have begun to model their behavior in the image of the best features of the minority community, while some blacks strive to imitate the worst features of the majority community. The Jewish population, for example, had among its eminent people listed in *Who's Who* only 12 percent who were educators in 1924 and 1925; this proportion was only half as large as the 23 percent educators among blacks listed in *Who's Who* at that time. In recent years (within the past decade), the university world became the most important source of eminence for Jewish people; 46 percent of the Jewish biographies in *Who's Who* were professional educators. This proportion was larger than that of any other group, including blacks, who dropped from a high of 52 percent educators between 1944 and 1945 to a recent low of 19 percent. During the fifty years between 1925 and 1975, Jews and blacks reversed their positions so far as education is concerned as a source of eminence. In 1925, proportionately twice as many blacks as Jews listed in *Who's Who* were educators; in 1975, proportionately twice as many Jews as blacks listed in *Who's Who* were educators (Lieberson and Carter 1979:359). It would appear that Jewish-Americans, who are white, are beginning to act like blacks, and Afro-Americans, who are black, are beginning to act like whites, fulfilling the observations of Polybius (200-118 B.C.).

Blacks once led in identifying education as a source of eminence in U.S. society. They are now becoming ambivalent and are turning away from their unique treasure as others are beginning to find it. Education—especially higher education—continues to be a major factor in the progress of both black and of white society. And this one should not forget: education is the only hedge that the meek and the minority have against the possibility of oppression by the mighty and the majority. The capacity to think can never be seized or stolen.

Education, driven by school desegregation, has had a beneficial effect for minorities and for all others. Rather than change our approach, we need to intensify our efforts so that the reforms that are less than three decades old may be brought to a successful conclusion of full participation by all at all levels of our system of education. The reforms in education that have come to pass would not have happened without the ambiguous impetus of desegregation—a process about which society remains ambivalent.

In summary, our nation is experiencing both the best of times and the worst of times in education in the opinion of some observers. The facts that follow indicate that these are good times:

Of all school-age children in the United States, 90 to 95 percent are registered on school rolls. We have almost achieved universal education at the elementary and secondary levels.

More than two-thirds of the adult population over twenty-five years of age are high school graduates.

Between the black and the white races of this nation, the difference in median school years completed is less than 1 percent.

Of all high school graduates, 50 percent go on to some form of postsecondary education; one-third go on to college.

Discrimination against women in higher education is abating. College no longer is a male preserve. One out of every two students in college is female; in many schools women are a majority.

Black women are leading the way in graduate education. Of all women college graduates, a higher proportion are black women.

Despite these accomplishments, we, like Pharoah of ancient history, attempt to deny the signs of the time; we harden our hearts and make an ambivalent response. That is precisely what is happening during the final quintile of this century of great educational change.

We have been told by high government authority that school desegregation, which brought equity and equality of access to education, is a failure. We have been told that our universal system of education, which sends half its graduates to postsecondary learning experiences and which has eliminated disparity in the median years of schooling completed by majority and minority races—which embraces handicapped students and those for whom English is a second language—which achieves these marvelous goals is mediocre, and that those who participate in it are greatly at risk of becoming underachievers.

Many of us have accepted these diagnoses, have begun to harden our hearts and search for ways of excluding those for whom the educational system has become increasingly open. We do this supposedly to protect the standards of our system. In reality, we harm ourselves by excluding others. For this reason, I state that this also is the worst of times for education.

Thus, it does not surprise me that during these good times in education, the nation has begun to make a bad response. History reminds us that evolution is not inevitable so far as human society is concerned. Modern history reminds us that those who are the brightest and the best are capable of acting the ugliest and the worst. Germany comes to mind as an example. It had some of the finest theologians, scientists, and artists. A society that nurtured the development of these qualities in its population nurtured atittudes that resulted in the Holocaust. The ancient history of Rome reminds us that when the movement for freedom and equality is passed on to the children and grandchildren of the founders, the new generation, having grown accustomed to these, no longer treasure them and begin to strive for preeminence. Such striving is antithetical to freedom and equality. This is Polybius' diagnosis of what happened to the Roman empire, of what contributed to its fall.

What was observed in ancient Rome is beginning to appear now in the United States. I refer specifically to the excellence movement in education. It is a subtle way of attempting to turn this system, which has become increasingly inclusive, into a system that is more exclusive.

We know that education is good and that in human society one cannot have too much of a good thing. The more people who are healthy, the better off is society at large. The more people who are educated, the better off are we all. Our nation has been reluctant to believe this fact.

REFERENCES

Dentler, Robert A. 1984. "The Boston School Desegregation Plan." In Charles Vert Willie, *School Desegregation Plans That Work*, pp. 59-80. Westport, Conn.: Greenwood Press.

Du Bois, W. E. B. 1935. *Black Reconstruction in America*. New York: Atheneum, 1969.

Hawley, Willis D. 1981. "Increasing the Effectiveness of School Desegregation: Lessons from the Research." In Adam Yarmolinsky, Lance Liebman, and Corinne S. Schelling, eds., *Race and Schooling in the City*, pp. 145-62. Cambridge, Mass.: Harvard University Press.

Jacobs, Jane. 1970. *The Economy of Cities*. New York: Vintage Books.

Lieberson, Stanley, and Donna K. Carter. 1979. "Making It in America." *American Sociological Review* 44 (June):347-66.

National Center for Education Statistics. 1982. *Digest of Education Statistics 1982*. Washington, D.C.: U.S. Government Printing Office.

Polybius. 200-118 B.C. In Ian Scott-Kilvert, trans., *Polybius: The Rise of the Roman Empire*. New York: Penguin Books, 1980.

Stanley, Manfred. 1978. *The Technological Conscience*. New York: Free Press.

von Euler, Mary. 1981. Foreword to Charles Vert Willie and S. L. Greenblatt, eds., *Community Politics and Educational Change*. New York: Longman.

Wharton, Clifton R., Jr. 1972. "Reflections on Black Intellectual Power." *Education Record* (Fall): 281-86.

Willie, Charles Vert. 1978. *The Sociology of Urban Education*. Lexington, Mass.: Lexington Books.

Index

About the Author

CHARLES VERT WILLIE is Professor of Education and Urban Studies in the Graduate School of Education at Harvard University. His most recent books include *Black and White Families, School Desegregation Plans That Work* (Greenwood Press, 1984), *Race, Ethnicity, and Socioeconomic Status,* and *The Sociology of Urban Education*. His latest articles have been published in *Equity and Choice* and *Phi Delta Kappan*.

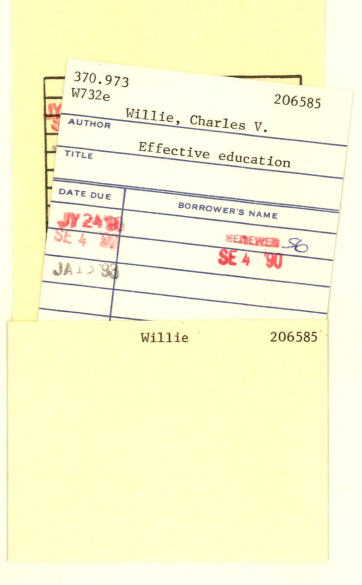